BREAKING THE SILENCE...

Reminiscences of a Hidden Child

By

Paul A. Schwarzbart

authorHOUSE

1663 LIBERTY DRIVE, SUITE 200
BLOOMINGTON, INDIANA 47403
(800) 839-8640
www.authorhouse.com

First published by AuthorHouse 08/06/04

ISBN: 1-4184-0712-7 (e)
ISBN: 1-4184-0711-9 (sc)

Library of Congress Control Number: 2004094708

Printed in the United States of America
Bloomington, Indiana

This book is printed on acid-free paper.

When I was the Rabbi of the Jewish community of Berlin under the Hitler regime, I learned many things. The most important thing I learned in my life and under those tragic circumstances is that bigotry and hatred are not the most urgent problems. The most urgent, the most shameful and the most tragic problem is silence.

Rabbi Joachim Prinz

The past must not overcome the present,
though its shadows both validate that present
and help shape the future...
(Paul A. Schwarzbart, 2003)

To the blessed memory of my dear Parents

Friedrich (Fritz) Schwarzbart
(1902-1945)

and

Sara Ryfka (Sidi) Schneider Schwarzbart
(1908-1969)

With my profoundest love, gratitude and respect

Table of Contents

I.

"Farewell, my Paulinka. I love you!" "Goodbye, my dearest Papa... I love you so!" I kiss my father's face and hands, separated from him by the wrought iron rungs of the police courtyard gate in Anderlecht, rue Georges Moreau. I then watch him tenderly kiss my mother, as best they can, given the bars. We shall never lay eyes on him again. Perhaps mercifully, my mother and I don't know that, and most certainly neither does he. It is Friday, May 10, 1940, the first day of the war for us in Brussels, and my father is under Belgian arrest for being Austrian -- ironically a privilege his country of birth denies him, for back "home" he is nothing more than ein Jude!, ein Untermensch! -- a Jew, not quite a human being...

That very morning we had awakened to pandemonium in the streets below, people rushing about every which way. Huge crowds, sheer and utter chaos. Black dots in the sky. Men being called up to rejoin their regiments. WAR: THE "BOCHES" ARE COMING! Later that morning, a persistent and loud knocking on our combination bedroom-living room door. Belgian police, gleaming white helmets and black capes. Some plainclothesmen too. Papers, sheaves of paper. "Friedrich Schwarzbart! In the name of the King, you are under arrest, as a potential enemy of the Belgian State. Your country (of origin) is at war with us. You must immediately accompany us!" We were dumbfounded and completely beside ourselves. What had we just heard? Was it real? Or was it a bad dream? It was real: they went on to inform us that

1

he would immediately be taken to the Rue Georges Moreau police station. We were allowed, perhaps even encouraged, to come there and bring him some spare clothing. And without further ado down the stairs they marched, surrounding my poor forlorn-looking Papa. After composing herself with the greatest difficulty, Mutti made up the suggested bundle. Papa's best suit (why, for God's sake, why?), shirts, underwear, socks, shoes. And handkerchiefs, of course, ample handkerchiefs. We rushed to the police station, only a few streets away.

And that bundle was ever so painstakingly squeezed, pushed and pulled between the bars into his waiting hands...

Papa softly admonishes me not to worry, that he will return as soon as this "gross mistake" is discovered, for a gross mistake it must indeed turn out to be; in the meantime, however, I am the man of the family and have to take good care of Mutti until he can, once again, resume his rightful responsibilities as head of our family. The little man he is thus addressing had just turned seven, not quite a month ago, but I should most assuredly protect my mother. So much love in his beautiful dark eyes, so much courage in his handsome face. And so much disbelief. No visible tears. The enormity of the occurrence undoubtedly escapes all of us, for who can truly comprehend what is actually happening here? We have been temporarily separated before, but no one in his right mind could have anticipated or even imagined the ramifications of this particular nightmare. No true precedent exists. We are Jews fleeing the Germans, fleeing for our lives. How can my dear father be arrested for anything, let alone as an anti-Belgian Germanophile, possibly even a fifth columnist? And untold thousands along with him, victims of the same horrible and irrevocable blunder. Sheer madness! It's all a terrible, terrible mistake, and the Belgian authorities will realize it presently, won't they? No indeed! They will not. Instead, they will compound the atrocity, in close complicity with their more-than-willing neighbors, the French. But what for now? Mother is absolutely despondent, I can readily tell. But she holds back her sobs, though she is deeply shaken and visibly shaking. My God, she is so very beautiful, so very sad. I truly don't know what to make of the situation, but I rely on her, as always. She will know. I am but seven years old, after all. And the spiral of death is spinning dizzily, irrevocably, pitilessly.

And so, having said our sad, sad goodbyes, alas our very last, we head for the nearest Red Cross office to make our inquiries. One pitiful aspect of war is endless people making endless inquiries about the endless absent or missing. And there we happen upon one Andrée Fricke-Exsteen, a very stern school teacher, imposing, tall, wearing impressive high riding boots. A teacher of German at the prestigious École Marius Renard, it turns out. She doesn't know much more than we do at this juncture, least of all where these wretched men are being sent--indeed, it is likely that no one does at that moment--but she suggests we speak further later that afternoon at her family home: 8, rue Émile Carpentier, a mere block away from our own address. Fortuitous. And thus we are plunged into the midst of her family: Madame Fricke, her aging mother. Matronly, warm and friendly. Georges, her architect husband. Courteous, but somewhat distant, perhaps shy or very private. Introverted. Just a glimpse of his study, to the left of the main entrance, a sealed refuge, his inner sanctum. Albert Fricke, one of Andrée's two brothers, a huge, affable man. Subsequently we are to meet her other brother too, Ernest, also an architect, who lives near the Anderlecht city hall, Place du Conseil. I never felt close to him or his wife Jeanne (they eventually moved away to Léopoldville, sometime after the war, and we lost track of one another completely; their choice, I think). And of course the children: Anne-Marie and little Jo-jo (Georges Jr.), both much younger than myself. And so Madame Exsteen talks with Mutti, at great length. I look around me, in total wonder. A lovely home, palatial to this young refugee's eyes, with absolutely gorgeous furnishings and the very latest amenities. A full balcony opening onto the street. French doors everywhere. Even a gorgeous backyard garden. Truly the very height of luxury, I think to myself. Returning there in the fifties, I find that everything has shrunk or has become tarnished, lost its freshness, its grandeur; even that garden I admired so much has become nothing more than a sad, tiny courtyard with barely any vegetation. The sheer pitiless unkindness of those few passing years is staggering... So much for the eyes of a child--or perhaps memory. The Exsteens propose that my mother come to work for them, to help rear the children and keep house for the family. A God-sent situation: food and perhaps a small income. All is not completely lost, at least for the time being. Someone cares and extends a hand in friendship. We grab on, with all of our might, as one does when falling, or to keep from being swept away or engulfed in a nightmare. Falling, falling, falling... Spinning, spinning, spinning...

But where is Papa meanwhile, is he passably well, how is he being treated, and when will he be returned to us to take his rightful place beside us again? Our hearts do ache so, but we know that Papa will rejoin us--he must! We hope with all our hearts: soon, very soon; perhaps today or tomorrow, or next week. Mutti and I constantly and fervently shore up that thought, one for the other, with every shred of positive news. Without that hope, there is only absolute and total void... Without hope there can be no life, no going on, nothing at all. But foremost and above all, we must survive! It is our duty. No, it is our responsibility... For we must be there for him when he returns.

Today, some sixty years later, I make every attempt possible within me to harbor no bitterness toward the irresponsible actions of the Belgian authorities. In my heart of hearts, I do want to believe that it was not an anti-Semitic move on their part, rather a knee-jerk reaction to the outside threat, be it unthinking and so incredibly devoid of feeling; simply another sad example of bureaucratic stupidity, or is that redundant? We Jews were, after all, refugees, strangers, no one about whom they really needed to care... Strict obedience to the law had forced us to register with their police, which only facilitated all that followed. Their unilateral action cost so many, many lives and completely altered so many, many more, hopelessly ruining them all--for ever. But I do hope against hope that it was neither willful nor calculated. It couldn't possibly have been planned that way--or could it? The entire world was so set against us though, even to the point of conspiring with the Nazis: Switzerland, the US (FDR's directives to his secretary of State about quotas and special rules. The Saint Louis scandal. IBM's total involvement with the Nazis, designing computers for them, helping them round up and keep track of Jews throughout WWII, from the safety of New York City and even via "neutral" Geneva.) And what of the freedom-loving French, whose camps stood ready and waiting so willingly to confine thousands upon thousands prior to their deportation East and ensuing annihilation? It went far beyond collaboration: the French were the first to arrest children, even before the Nazis considered moving in that direction to victimize children too! 1,500,000

6

martyred children. Unthinkable? Surely, but real nonetheless. It did indeed happen! Have you ever visited the children's memorial at the Yad Vashem in Jerusalem??? Unforgettable, even if one were to live to be 120! I remember breaking down and sobbing, not for myself, but at the sudden thought that had my name been mentioned among the litany of names read in that dark hall, my beloved sons, Marc and David, would not grace this world with their beautiful presence.

On the other hand, but in a similar vein, I can find no viable excuses for the internment of the Japanese-Americans by their own countrymen; all the while the sons of these imprisoned families, the Nisei battalions, fought so gallantly in defense of freedom. Injustices are ever present--and seldom, if ever, righted. How can they be? I still see the tears welling up in the eyes of a San Francisco high school teacher of Japanese descent, as I mentioned these iniquities during one of my Holocaust presentations. No closure there.

Deep down though, in spite of everything past and present, I'm more of a realist than a cynic, I do believe... But rancor does well up occasionally, with a vengeance.

I do vividly remember kindness and compassion from almost everyone with whom we had any real contact in those ever-tense days. Even though Papa was interned as a "potential enemy", I recall no incident when we were made to feel blatantly unwelcome. More often than not, we were simply ignored, looked "through" at times. Lonely, very lonely days. Everything was in chaos, of course, and total bewilderment reigned predominantly. We all knew that the German hordes were relentlessly and inevitably marching toward us, but how soon would they trample us underfoot? Our family and other Jewish friends were desperately frightened and uncertain, but literally no one dared propose a course of action. We all "simply" waited for events to run their course. Unimaginable, really, as I sit here, pondering, writing. Mutti and I were lucky in many respects, for we had the friendship and tacit support of family, of the Exsteens, and of a few other dear friends and acquaintances.

From our bedroom window we could look straight down rue Émile Carpentier, right to the corner where stood my massive school, l'École Communale No. 9, and across from its imposing structure, at 89 rue Éloy, the tall apartment building filled with Jewish families of our acquaintance. There we spent long hours with my uncle Poldi's (Leopold) parents and siblings, the Stör family.

They were fur jobbers in Brussels, meaning that they made piles of rabbit fur mittens in their tiny apartment. Not always an appetizing aroma, fresh fur; it made me gag. I was quite fond of the elder Störs, whom I had not known in Vienna at all. To me they were very, very old indeed. I truly believe that the whole family liked us too, since my father was the only brother of my uncle's wife, my aunt Herta. I also know that it was a link with "home" to which my poor mother and the others clung fiercely and almost with desperation. Mutti and I gave each other enormous love and affection, but she had little else. She was sustained solely by her profound belief that Papa would return to us, and that we would be a family once again, and as happy as before. That went far beyond rational imagination. Ignorance, the simple reality of not knowing, can indeed be bliss -- given the wrong circumstances. But "before" would never be again, ever...

II.

    Our Anderlecht neighborhood was overrun with military personnel. Belgian, of course, but also French and British. So many uniforms and strange war paraphernalia. Troops were billeted everywhere and also in my school, and hence we were, my classmates and I, also deprived of that safe haven during those few interminable days. Mutti and I spent our time visiting the Störs and the Exsteens. The two of us had our portraits taken, Chaussée de Mons, I think, to send to Papa eventually.

The Exsteens encouraged these seemingly useless "keep busy" activities; I believe they wanted to prevent us from just moping and going stir-crazy. Intelligent and compassionate.

We were discouraged enough, however, and everyone seemed to fuel that feeling of despair in others. Only the very arrogant German Jews, the Jekkes as we called them, appeared less despondent, because in their view they had very little to fear: "Hitler would not come after us, since we are Germans!" Distinctions indeed! Poor, poor wretched fools! Though we all disliked them heartily and intensely at that time, they were soon to suffer every Jew's fate; for we all certainly found out in short order that the Nazis really didn't care or distinguish. Vermin is vermin, after all! Untermenschen, one and all... Such a cruel wake-up call.

Somehow the Belgians did seem less traumatized than we, as I vaguely remember. Fewer past experiences, I wager, but also strong pro-German sentiments particularly on the part of the Flemish contingent, those frightful and frightening collaborators who later became the Black Shirts under the occupation, and who were even more cruel and zealous than the Germans themselves. After all, they did have to "prove" themselves worthy of their new protectors and mentors, didn't they?

So, between the uncertainty of my father's whereabouts and condition and our own precarious future, we were on a constant emotional roller coaster, prey to whatever bits of news surfaced or were rumored. I felt like a little old man of seven and was of course expected to act very grown-up. Childhood, as others know it, had been short-lived and was gone, forever. That is, until the birth of my two sons, so many years later, when I gleefully recaptured some of its aspects...

A painstakingly slow week goes by. On Saturday morning, May 18, we are awakened by the profound and unbroken silence in the streets. My mother goes to the window. Not a cat to be seen below. The school's huge portals gape open, wide. Empty, quite empty. Our "defenders" have run off during the night. The beginning of the retreat, the "grande débâcle". Mutti knowingly and dejectedly utters "Now the Germans will be here at any moment!" We get dressed and cross over to the Stör's apartment building, 89 rue Eloy, and there we all huddle near the windows and wait, hardly speaking, anxious, fearful, short of breath. That morning does indeed stand out in my memory for its long, eerie, chilling silence. And then, that silence is suddenly shattered by the sound of heavy motors, and a column of German vehicles appears, military police at the intersection below, red discs in hand, silver half-moon on the chest, directing the flow. Interminable black on white German crosses (Wehrmachtskreuze or Balkenkreuze), and interminable swastikas! German steel helmets--unmistakable and unforgettable--many more helmets than faces it seems. To this day I cannot abide them, and motorcyclists wearing

11

replicas or the real thing painted black makes me shudder still. What makes these so horribly appealing to these insensitive people? Even the Darth Vader figure is reminiscent of that time to me! The sheer number of hated symbols of Teutonic oppression is staggering. Their sheer number is staggering. Everything is staggering. But not a shot, practically no other sounds, just the relentless and systematic ooze of Nazi occupation. The scales of life are tilted, out of balance. From freedom to enslavement in barely a few moments. Spiraling, spiraling...

      What follows is the drudgery of occupation. L'heure allemande. Displayed everywhere "Avis" in French, Flemish and German, informing the population of the new rules and regulations to be obeyed to the letter or suffer the dire consequences. Simple and relatively logical mundane matters at first: food rationing (long, dismal queues in front of the food stores), curfews, general submissive behavior. Quite an elaborate and well-planned campaign: the people were to be slowly and thoroughly anesthetized, lulled into a completely false feeling of security or at least the absence of immediate danger. And it worked very well indeed on the masses. I remember people saying to us: "Things aren't really so bad, after all. What were you Jews talking about? The Germans aren't monsters. You can readily see that now, can't you?" Until their own turn came... Pastor Martin Niemöller, himself a German, expressed it best, as I remember: "First they came for the Jews. I was silent. I was not a Jew. Then they came for the Communists. I was silent. I was not a Communist. Then they came for the trade unionists. I was silent. I was not a trade unionist. Then they came for me. There was no one left to speak for me." Does anyone else remember? Do enough remember, ever?

It was a strange routine to settle into. But oddly enough, within a few weeks that's exactly what it did indeed become, a routine. When school finally reopened, my day was pretty much planned out for me. Mutti spent her time at the Exsteens, working unbelievably hard, literally slaving. And this is absolutely no reflection on the Exsteens. Rearing two children and keeping house for so many people was far from being a sinecure. And Andrée was a taskmaster, a benevolent tyrant. As for me, I did suddenly have trouble concentrating in class, though I fully understood the importance of my promise to my father. He was ever-present in my mind and I can only imagine the heaviness of Mother's heart. Perhaps physical labor is more numbing, thus possibly more endurable, than mental endeavors, but I know that those times were very, very difficult for us both. So much uncertainty, not only about Papa, which was more than enough, but our own survival too. Everything was so tentative. Late evening was the best and worst time, when she and I could talk, and weep, and hope, and wait. And the waiting went on... The Exsteens would occasionally share BBC information with us, but essentially we were very much in the dark. I think they kept much from us, though. The outside world, the free world, was far, far away, quite out of reach, closed off to us. We were so incredibly much alone, so utterly abandoned. But never completely hopeless.

III.

Some two months later, Papa's first letter reaches us. It is dated July 26, 1940. He is incarcerated in the Pyrénées Orientales, at the French camp of St. Cyprien. New names to learn, another lesson in geography--tentative, to be sure, for we had no maps, no direct references. 15 more letters follow from the same detention center, the last one dated October 20.

Then letter #17 bears the stamp of Gurs (Basses Pyrénées) and is dated October 30. Where is that forsaken place? According to Henri Martin (Journal d'un détenu politique à Gurs, 1940), another detainee at this most infamous camp, in Gurs the prisoners endure, aside from captivity, scores of humiliations, promiscuity, the hatred and cruelty of the French guards, vermin, the lack of hygiene, sickness, hunger, pain, bitter cold, and even death... I recently viewed a 54' documentary by Jean-Jacques Mauroy entitled Mots de Gurs, de la guerre d'Espagne à la Shoah, which sheds some light on that dismal French internment camp. Papa is to remain in Gurs until the fall of 1941, when letter #55 is written to us on September 12. Letter #56, dated September 19, 1941, arrives from the 3rd French camp, Savigny (Haute Savoie, Pyrénées), where he remains until August 1942, letter #97 dated August 18. Letter #98, August 21, is from the transit camp of Ruffieux. It is followed by letter #99, his very last note, thrown off a train leaving the Gare de Lyon and posted to us by some anonymous good Samaritan, most likely a Quaker, for I have read that the Friends endeavored to help that way. The date on that very brief goodbye note is August 24, 1942. It's what appears at first to be a rather matter-of-fact note, but the love and care are very much in evidence; after all, he didn't know who would find and read it. Essentially it says "I'm being shipped East, and I'll write again at the first opportunity. Keep up your faith: God will provide. With many kisses, your Papa Fritz". Ninety-nine letters of hope and love, so much hope, so much love. Two days later, on 26 August 1942, he was deported from Le Bourget Drancy to Auschwitz as Jude No. 179475. The beginning of his ultimate journey, albeit a drawn out and desperate one. Slavery, torture, abject and unfathomable misery. We are never to hear from him again. Spinning, spinning, spinning… Falling, falling, falling… Spinning, spinning, spinning…

These horrible and unnecessary deportations were enthusiastically instigated by Pierre Laval, the Vichy president under Pétain (summarily hanged after the Libération by his country's hasty justice, most likely to prevent him from implicating so many others just as responsible for France's deeply deserved shame) and just as enthusiastically carried out by Vichy's despicable minions.

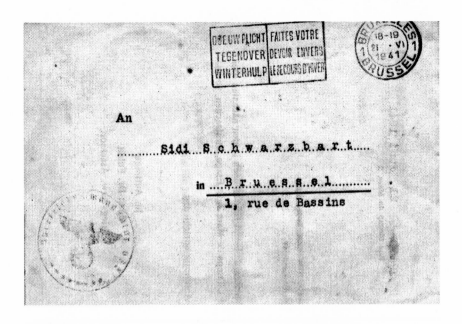

An

Sidi Schwarzbart

in Bruessel

1, rue de Bassins

OBEUW PLICHT | FAITES VOTRE
TEGENOVER | DEVOIR ENVERS
WINTERHULP | LE SECOURS D'HIVER

Oberfeldkommandantur 672
    Verwaltungschef

Ref. 5 Verkehr.

Brüssel, den 21. Juni 1941
Rue Champ de Mars, 2

Betr.: ~~Verstoss gegen die Kraftfahrzeugsanmelde-Bestimmungen. Kraftwagen-Nr.~~

Sie werden ersucht, ~~~~ in den nächsten drei Tagen vormittags zwischen 9 und 12 Uhr, rue du Champs de Mars 2, II* Etage, Strafsachen, vorzusprechen.

Falls Sie nicht erscheinen, wird ohne Ihre Anhörung entschieden.

Im Auftrage :
Gez.: Dr. Fulda
Kriegsverw. Assessor.

Oberfeldkommandantur 672

5. Verkehr post.

Str. L ....X..S..10......

Brüssel, den ....5.Juli 1941......
Rue Champ de Mars 2, II. Etage

An Sidi SCHWARZBART

B r ü s s e l
rue de Barsins 1

STRAFVERFÜGUNG

Auf Grund der Verordnung über die Polizeistrafgewalt der Ortskommandanten vom 18.5.1940 in Verbindung mit der Verordnung über den Nachrichtenverkehr vom 2. 4. 1940 und den Ausführungsbestimmungen hierzu werden Sie mit einer Geldstrafe von ....500..... bfrs. (in Worten : ....fünfhundert......... bfrs.) bestraft.

Die Geldstrafe ist binnen einer Woche nach Zustellung dieses Bescheides bei der Zahlmeisterei der O.F.K. Brüssel, Place du Trône 1, Zimmer 3 (vormittags zwischen 9-12 Uhr) einzuzahlen. Bei Nichtzahlung tritt an die Stelle eine Ersatzfreiheitsstrafe von ....10............ Tagen Haft.

GRÜNDE

Durch Feststellung der Auslandsbriefprüfstelle haben Sie durch einen Brief vom ..8.4.41. den Verkehr mit Personen in ...unbesetzte Frankreich............aufzunehmen versucht.

Rechtsmittelbelehrung

Gegen diese Strafverfügung können Sie binnen 24 Stunden nach Bekanntgabe bei meiner Dienststelle Beschwerde einlegen. Durch die Beschwerde wird die sofortige Strafvollstreckung nicht aufgeschoben. Im Wiederholungsfalle haben Sie mit einer erheblich höheren Strafe zu rechnen.

Im Auftrage:
gez.: Dr. F u l d a
Kriegsverw.Assessor.

Beglaubigt

Kriegsverw.Sekr.

Druck : Arbeitsstab für Karten- u. Vermessungswesen. - Brüssel.

Oberfeldkommandantur 672
    Ref. 5 Verkehr
      Str. L. *Σ. S. 10*
                             O.U., den 24.Juli 1941

               An

                .....Sidi Schwarzbart.................

               ....rue de Berpini 2...............

                     B r ü s s e l

       Auf Jhren Antrag von   wird die Strafe von
.........500..... bfrs. auf ...150......... bfrs. festgesetzt.
Die Einzahlung hat nunmehr sofort zu erfolgen, da andernfalls
die Ermaessigung wieder aufgehoben wird.

                                    J. A.
                              Kriegsverwaltungsrat.

On June 21, 1941, Mutti receives a summons from the Brussels Oberfeldkommandatur, Rue Champ de Mars 2, second floor, addressed to her by her nickname Sidi, not by her name, Sara! Whoever this is, Sidi or Sara Schwarzbart, she must appear. Chapter and verse. There is no alternative, and into the lions' den she ventures. I wait at home, impotent and frightened. Much later that day she returns, still ashen. She will "simply" be fined 500 Belgian Francs for attempting to communicate with unoccupied France on April 8, 1941. She had dared write to Vichy-ruled France, the Germans' partners in crime, where my poor father is being held! Grossly inhuman and calculated harassment, which surely contributed in shortening her life span. The notice of punishment finally arrives, dated July 5, 1941. But she appeals the stated fine! How? By what courage and on what grounds? On July 24, 1941, another communication from that very Oberfeldkommandatur summarily reduces the formerly stated punishment amount to 150 Belgian Francs, payable immediately or else. I don't really know how she manages, it's a huge sum, but pay she does. And where in Heaven's name did that dear lady find the "guts" to stand up to the frightful German war machine and its extraordinary and petty red tape? And to do so, successfully...

Apparently the French allowed brief conjugal furloughs for some of their prisoners who could somehow manage to get home, and for whom another prisoner would offer his own life as guarantee for his prompt return to the camp. It appears that Joshi Blau, Grete Stör's husband, convinced Papa to be such a guarantor and to vouch for him... And so Joshi came home to his family, ostensibly for a brief visit.

Unfortunately for my father, Joshi never fulfilled his promise to return to Gurs. By sacrificing himself as guarantor, Fritz forfeited any chance of being granted a similar "leave of absence" by the French and therefore never saw us again; afterwards my mother was always quite bitter about my father's selfless action, which he disclosed to us in one of his letters. He was of course absolutely certain that Joshi would keep his word to him. But Joshi rather remained in Brussels with his wife and the Störs. Alas, he was subsequently ensnared with Grete at the 89, rue Eloy, ANDERLECHT, address in 1942; they were both deported on Convoy III (numbers 386 and 213 respectively,) and went to their deaths together. And indirectly so did Fritz.

I'm sure there are many such sad and unfortunate incidents, but this one really touches me even more profoundly. I shall never know that poor man's thoughts or reasons, and we shouldn't necessarily impugn his motives. But the "situation" certainly lengthened Papa's hard road to death. What if?... Perhaps?... Who can say?... I don't think Mutti ever forgave Joshi, though she was never really privy to all the wretched details I have unearthed a mere few years ago.

Anderlecht. On a crowded streetcar, the 56 or the 22, I can't recall exactly. A snot-nosed young blackshirt, a real skinhead, is forcing his presence on us, arrogantly, sneeringly. An old gentleman, most likely a WWI veteran, rebukes him sharply in French, pointing out the shame of wearing "that" uniform in his own country. "Have you no pride as a Belgian?" The "kid" draws his pistol and shoots the old man dead, as though he were a rabid dog, very matter-of-factly. Had he spoken Flemish--who knows? The militia man blows his whistle to stop the streetcar and call for the police. We hurriedly get off before they arrive. It can only mean trouble. No one looks at the smirking murderer, or even at the corpse, for fear of suffering a similar fate. There certainly is no accountability for the perpetrator. The gun rules. And they are clearly above the law. "They" have every right. We Untermenschen, however, have none.... Had he suspected I am a Jew, God only knows. Following May or June 1942, after we were made to wear the six-pointed Yellow Star over our heart, we didn't ride too often anymore. But for now, this day at least, safe for another moment...

IV.

May 12, 1943. One month ago today, I turned ten. A knock at the bedroom door, but a rather discreet one. Not like the police who came for my father, already three long years ago. He is young, late teens or very early twenties at most. He calls us by name, very politely, very directly, very straightforwardly matter-of-fact, but not unfeeling. "The current situation in Brussels is becoming untenable. If you want to save your son's life, Madame, you must let me take him away! Will you?" What an incredible question for a mother to hear. "We shall hide him from the Nazis, we shall keep him safe. But you must not ask where. You may not know." We are both absolutely dumbfounded and completely thrown off balance. The visit is so absolutely unexpected. When Mutti regains her composure, she asks him whether she may have some time to make up her mind. He can give her a couple of hours, no more, and he will return later for her decision. And so the two of us hurry over to the Exsteens and relate what has just transpired. The family consults, feverishly. They are obviously much more aware of current events than we are, and they unhesitatingly tell my mother: "Faites-le, Madame Schwarzbart!" "Do it, Mrs. Schwarzbart!" and they so very altruistically offer me the use of their surname, for I need a new identity. Au revoir! perhaps... They must realize that they would share my fate, were I to be caught. No matter. It just needed doing. Can one ever be thankful enough? Today, I wonder how much they actually did know. When the young man returns later on, Mutti nods and tells him simply "Yes!". My backpack

23

is ready, as is hers, right by the door. They have been there for months, in readiness: the Germans demand that they not be made to wait, when they come for you, and personal belongings are to be packed. Mother makes me wear my best shoes, the new pair, of course. Since June of 1942, a Yellow Star with a centered "J" (so very practically standing for Juif, Jood or Jude) had to be displayed on the chest under penalty of death; and so I am of course wearing the infamous "étoile jaune". So huge on my little chest. One of the last things Mutti does for me as I am getting ready to go into exile, is to rip it from my clothing. Except for the tip of my circumcised penis, I am now unidentifiable as a Jew--if I keep my mouth shut and my pants up! Paul Schwarzbart is fading into the shadows and Paul Exsteen, Belgian and soon to be a devoutly practicing Catholic, is emerging... But not really displacing him. My first engagement, and a starring role at that! We kiss goodbye and cling to each other; goodbye or adieu forever? It must be tearing that wonderful heart right out of her breast, that seemingly simple "Yes!" So much love, so much courage, such selflessness. Will she ever see her Pauli again? What is to become of her? She stands there, so alone, so forlorn, so stoical, a barely breathing statue. And then I walk out the door, the young résistant holding me by the hand, and down the three flights of stairs to the street. No looking back. Darkness has fallen, the streets are a violet blue. Hazy. We take a streetcar to the Luxembourg train station. "Remember well, you're not Jewish" he whispers. He accompanies me to my train, tells me that it will be a long all-night journey, that in the morning I should watch for the name of "Jamoigne" and get off there, wishes me luck and shakes my hand, man to man, then he turns and disappears into the crowd. We shall never meet again. I am exactly ten years and one month old, but I am expected to behave as would a man. And somehow I muster what it takes to do just that.

The young resistance fighter was quite right, it was long. A crowded train, but I was all the more so very much alone, so afraid, so lonely, so uncertain, so confused... Where was I going and why? What would happen to me there? What would be happening to Mutti, all alone in Anderlecht? What was happening to Papa meanwhile? I did not sleep; though terribly weary I was at the same time so wary of everyone and everything. And in the morning, at one of the very frequent stops, there indeed and at long last appeared the sign "Jamoigne".

And so I grabbed my backpack and quickly jumped off the train. I was obviously easy to spot, for a tall young man, with a huge mane of hair and wearing some kind of uniform with shorts, approached me and quietly inquired whether my name was Paul Exsteen. I replied in the affirmative, and he introduced himself as Akéla, a teacher at the school to which I had been sent. So, I was going to a school. He was very amiable, outgoing, even compassionate. He could see my bewilderment and tried to comfort me, assuring me that this school for boys was a very good one, that I would have lots of comrades and would readily make friends, and that all in all I'd be quite happy to find myself there. By a strange coincidence, his real name was Pol. Different spelling, almost identical pronunciation. We started off toward the school. It turned out to be a very long trek indeed. My new shoes were pinching me mercilessly, and we both had a good laugh at their expense. My poor feet. I was unaccustomed to walking with someone who took pretty long strides. But it helped to keep my mind off more important matters. We crossed the village, tiny and very rural, and came to a big wrought iron gate, leading into an avenue bordered by large oak-like trees.   Very grand.

This led to a huge lawn, and there, facing us squarely, squatted an immense château!   Four corner turrets, massive, overwhelming to a frightened, though curious, little boy.   Wow, what's this?! Another first.   We made our way through a side entrance and along some beautiful hallways paneled in dark wood.   We finally reached wide steps leading up to very high and wide double doors. Reminded me of my school's entry, back there in Anderlecht. But that was on another planet, in another lifetime.

On the other side there was an "enormous" hall filled with boys standing around tables. Big and little. And adults too, mostly in shorts. And two or three women completely in black, with huge white headdresses covering their shoulders and even chests. Nuns, I was later informed. I could definitely smell food, and I was so incredibly hungry. A boy's appetite is apparently not spoiled by chagrin. But these boys were not eating. They were reciting things in a language I had never before heard. And then they all made a gesture with their right hand, first to the forehead, then to the belly, and finally to both shoulders. I had no idea as to what was going on, none whatsoever. At long last they all sat down to eat, and my companion led me to a vacant seat. Food! Reality sank in, with the help of a few well-placed but innocent-sounding questions: I had landed in a Catholic school, and what I had just witnessed so unwittingly, was the boys saying grace in Latin prior to crossing themselves! Chameleon-like miraculous overnight transformation: I was now a Belgian Catholic, and I had better learn to fit in quickly and without a hitch. Another challenge to be met, another lesson to assimilate: survival of the quick learner. Very quick, or else!

V.

Mimicking has always been one of my strengths. And so I mimicked everything, repeating without any real comprehension, gesturing without any real meaning, at first. With so many other boys to copy, I managed rather well. Altogether, there were 125 boys at the school, aged five to fourteen. During the period of heaviest attendance, there were 160. We were segregated by age, and so my immediate peer group was essentially nine-ten-eleven. Quite manageable. Our teaching staff followed the guidelines of Baden Powell and Rudyard Kipling's Jungle Books; we were therefore organized as cub-scouts, the older boys as full-fledged scouts, and the younger kids were called ducklings (les louveteaux, les scouts, les canards). Most ingenious and well thought out. The boys essentially helped to manage themselves, both physically and morally. And pedagogically sound. Akéla (Lion de Choc) turned

out to be in charge of the cubs, so he became my leader, my mentor, my surrogate father. I simply adored him. No prejudice: he was adorable! A born teacher and leader. And what a Mensch! He is unfortunately gone now, but not my deep love and respect for him.

Religion, Catholicism in point of fact, dominated our lives and marked our every waking moment. Naturally, we attended mass every morning, and naturally, everyone took holy communion. Every single second was a learning experience. So on the first morning there I knelt too, mouth agape, tongue stuck out. And l'Abbé René Elisée Hardy, the young twenty-eight year-old priest, placed a small white wafer on it. Tasteless. My first communion. That was God, I was told. Hard to swallow for a ten-year old... I say this with the greatest respect, no pun intended. But it was hard to swallow, in every regard. And the fact that the priest actually drank the blood of Christ. Smelled like wine, but it was transformed, I was again told. My poor little mind was reeling. But I never flinched and behaved like all the rest. Mustn't stand out, never stand out. I fully understood my responsibility to survive, I owed that to my parents, but I also understood that, were I to be caught, everyone, the other boys and the monitors, some thirty of them, would pay the price with me. The Germans were unforgiving: you help a Jew and you suffer his same fate. Couldn't let that happen, now could I? Pretty strong little rounded shoulders, pretty strong little back. A lot was indeed expected of me. And I gave a lot, but without belaboring the thought. And I received a lot in return.

Father Hardy also shepherded other youth groups in the neighboring villages, les Croisés (crusaders, bearers of the cross) and used to make his rounds on a motorcycle, holding onto his béret, his cassock filled with air rising on either side as he sped off noisily along our country roads amidst billows of smoke and dust... What an image! Forever and indelibly engraved. He loved cigars; ugh, what a stench. Wonder where he got them. Another Mensch indeed.

Nor shall I ever forget my initial confession. It must have been my very first week at the château. My group lined up, two by two, and off we marched down one on the long corridors. "Where are we going?" "Hey, you stupid or what?, it's Thursday, isn't it? Confession!" I wasn't at all sure what the word meant. But there was l'Abbé Hardy, right outside the chapel, sitting on a straight back chair. We stopped, the first boy in line went up to him, knelt and did his thing. Well, when my turn finally came I gave him exactly what the boy ahead of me had said and done. Without batting an eye he gave me absolution and penance. Not too much to confess, really. Could one be in a state of grace simply by being? What would have happened if there had been a real confessional, in which case I could not have overheard or seen anything of what went on? We'll never know, but I was resourceful. Suffice it to say that I played my role so well and learned so quickly, that within a couple of weeks the young priest made me his regular altar boy. And I served mass every day thereafter, low mass in the village convent's chapel at the crack of dawn.

(PIB) JAMOIGNE. — Pensionnat des Sœurs Ste-Marie.

I had to leave the château so early to make my way into the village, that I remember winter mornings when I'd have to break the surface ice of the cow trough near the main gate, to wash and get ready for mass properly. Cleanliness first and foremost, both moral and physical! I took my role most seriously and treated it with the greatest respect. No dogmatic problems, either. For once I became accustomed to the idea of the Trinity (instead of One God), the rest fell into place simply. After all, wasn't Jesus a Jew, too! And none of the teachings of upright behavior really clashed with anything I had learned before. On the contrary, they were reinforcements or perhaps even embellishments.

Our castle-school, the Château du Faing, was known to all as the Home Reine Elisabeth (the queen of Belgium). It was under the absolute control of Madame Marie Mertens Taquet

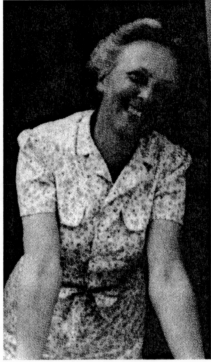

and her husband Émile Taquet, "the Major" to us.

Quite obviously his Belgian Army rank. Small and wiry, with a slight limp, he hardly ever smiled and was usually accompanied by one of his two dogs, Jeck and Whisky, the former a German shepherd, and "Gaspard" a malicious black crow. Most of us were a bit frightened of this quiet man, but we also respected him. As for "Maman Taquet" as we all called her, she was adored by all of us. Very strict but fair, she was indeed a "no-nonsense" administrator and ran the school with an iron fist inside a velvet glove. And what a job was hers. Feeding and clothing so many, all with rather scarce resources. But she was a terrific planner with a big, big heart. We called her "maman" because she was exactly that to us.

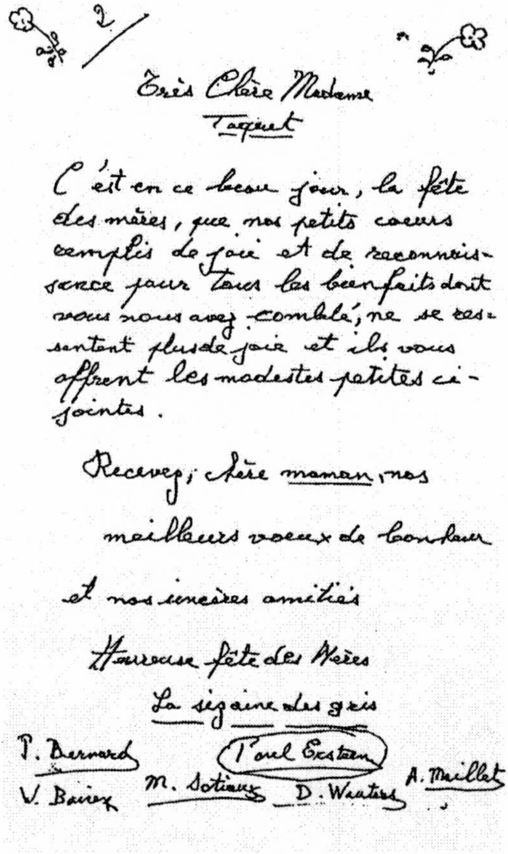

Très Chère Madame
Taquet

C'est en ce beau jour, la fête des mères, que nos petits cœurs remplis de joie et de reconnaissance pour tous les bienfaits dont vous nous avez comblé, ne se ressentent plus de joie et ils vous offrent les modestes petites ci-jointes.

Recevez, chère maman, nos

meilleurs vœux de bonheur

et nos sincères amitiés

Heureuse fête des Mères

La séraine des gris

P. Bernard   Paul Exstern   A. Maillet
V. Bairy   M. Sotiaux   D. Waaties

At night she'd go around to tuck the kids in, kissing us all good night--her famous "bisou". If she were detained we just wouldn't go to sleep. We'd wait until she could make her rounds. To me she was even more special, because I understood that she knew who I really was, intuitively. Nothing ever spoken though. Occasionally, she would surreptitiously slip me a raw egg, which I immediately, and just as surreptitiously sucked out of its shell as is. I still love eggs. But why me? For she loved us all, everyone of us. Later, so many years later, I found out indirectly that she and her husband, the Major, referred to me in particular as "the little Prince"…

Now and again other kids would ask me why I never received any mail. Not really intentionally mean, I think, rather naturally curious. I learned to fabricate elaborate white lies. I really don't recall exactly what I made up, but apparently it did satisfy my questioners' curiosity. Mail call was rough on me, for I knew not to expect anything--yet I did. Decades later, while serving my Uncle Sam so far away from home, I clearly remember looking forward to mail call with the same eagerness but much less frustration. Clearly, we desperately require direct links with our roots. It wasn't all that simple though. Modesty, for instance. It was a natural must, of course, so I never undressed completely or even took off my underpants in front of anyone. Never "swam" in the nude, for instance. Not all that difficult either, really. But an ever-present mandate. No reminders necessary. We were a Catholic school, after all. But Sister Marie-Madeleine (who ran the infirmary) must have known something, unless she (modestly) averted her eyes whenever vigorously "plunging in" with her infamous thermometer—which she dutifully accomplished at the slightest hint of illness! I don't believe any of that even occurred to me then...

Our days were very full and busy. Imagine the enormous task of constantly occupying 125 squirming kids! And with a war raging. As an educator, I can truly appreciate today what a daunting challenge faced the Taquets and their staff. But they took it all in stride.

The monitors were often late teenagers themselves, or barely in their early twenties, but to us they were "old" of course. They all had "totems" which are war names based quite often on the Kipling Jungle Books they followed.

Pol Georis, "Akéla" the old wolf (though his actual scouting totem was Lion de Choc) was my very favorite. "Fourmi" (Laurette Molle: ant), the lady who was to become his wife and the mother of some six children, was both beautiful and kind. There were also "Épervier" (Léonard Schmitz: sparrow-hawk), "Mouton" (Comblain Gordon: sheep), "Élan" (André Buyle: elk), "Antilope" (Jean-Marie Fox: antelope), "Bagheera" (Jean Hardy), "Picard" (Jacques Delvaux), "Gabriel" (Robert Delvaux), "Milet" (Pierre Delvaux), "Ponpon" (Marie-Thérèse Poncelet), etc... An entire rather esoteric ménagerie! Much easier, and much more exciting for us, than "real" names. Safer, too... Never crossed my mind.

We all slept in makeshift dormitories, of course, cots neatly aligned side by side. At times mine was squeezed inside one of the huge stone fireplaces, because I had been known to wet my bed, much to my dismay, and they wanted to safeguard the parquet floors! But most of the time I had a white plaster wall at my head, and I delighted in artistic embellishments, drawing scouting crosses and silhouettes above my bed. Pretty fair drawings, too, as I remember. At least Akéla thought so and complimented me, once we got the official nod of approval after-the-fact. I was only emulating him. The many drawings he made for me, still prize possessions today, were also very poetic... He was indeed wonderful in every respect. And truly gifted.

The three sisters of Charity (Soeurs de la Charité de Besançon, owners of the château since 1903) were Sister Marie-Madeleine (Van der Smissen) who was in charge of the infirmary and took such good care of all of us, though she was indeed a terror, more often than not brandishing her (anal) thermometer or a throat swab! Sister Marguerite-Marie (Ligier) who handled the farm's pigs and whom I remember with her sleeves rolled up to her elbows carrying pails of pig slop (she may have also worked in the "buanderie" the wash house, a small structure close to the pig sty, steam ever escaping), and older Sister François-Régis (Faivre), whom we reverently called Mère Supérieure (Mother Superior). In addition to our beloved chaplain, l'Abbé René Elisée Hardy, there was also the old priest, le Père François, who had a small cottage near the side entrance to the domaine. He said daily mass for the three sisters in the tiny chapel. And finally there was l'Abbé Boët, parish priest of the village, who seldom had anything to do with us but who subsequently did baptize me in the grand old church. We were prayed for and with, all the time. The "Pater Noster" and "Ave Maria" were a constant and integral part of our daily routine, and we had repeated occasions to pray with our chapelet (rosary beads) and to make the sign of the cross, be it as a group or alone. It was indeed a very full and complete way of life.

In the morning we'd traditionally have classes with various monitors. I always preferred Akéla, but then I readily admit to my deep and utter prejudice. All these young people valiantly tried to keep us abreast of our studies, and they succeeded remarkably well--since I was able to rejoin my regular class "afterwards" without any penalty. In the afternoon, following the obligatory naptime, we'd make our way to the woods, or to the bosquet behind the château. In the forests of Phaël and Grand Terme we had built huts in a clearing and established our cub scout camp, flagpole and all, gleaming white rocks to delineate the walkways. Impeccable. Absolutely grand in retrospect. One of my favorite games was to climb a "sapin" and then, by pulling the top of another one toward me, move gingerly from tree to tree. Fun, but I always ended up with a lot of pitch on me. Sticky! It taught me to climb quickly, which served me well when I had one of my very rare encounters with a wild boar. Also my very first taste of juicy blackberries and raspberries! Daily "roll call" was held behind the château, on the concrete slabs that once were the tennis courts. There we also sang the "Brabançonne" and saluted the tricolored (black, yellow, and red) Belgian flag.

Great morale booster! Streng Verboten though! Punishable by God-knows-what! (death--or worse…) Luckily for us, we didn't have the slightest inkling as to what "worse" could possibly mean... Living together at such close range taught us so much about getting along, how to make the necessary compromises and to become somewhat more self-effacing for the common good. The moral values taught by the scouting movement, along with the rigorous preachings of catechism, established a very firm character basis for us. The Judeo-Christian ethics were ever present, though the term "Judeo" was strictly non-existent: it was never mentioned or brought up. But I knew. I knew.

So, in this relative peace and semblance of normalcy, I also had to seem and act "normal" By day I was just another happy-go-lucky Belgian Catholic kid, going about my business of being reared properly and learning all I could about everything, running my little squad of cubs (I had become a leader, of course!) and quietly crying myself to sleep at night. What was happening to Papa, to Mutti, to the rest of my family? Would we ever be reunited? Yes, I was absolutely certain that sooner or later we would! That hope was the driving force of my existence. Luckily for me. But keeping up appearances can levy a heavy toll. Very silent, very private, very bitter tears.

I can clearly see myself on my way to the village to visit Akéla and Fourmi at their house that one day. It must be mid-morning, and I obviously have a special dispensation to be out and about. In the main street, I see what I immediately recognize as a German truck. The insignia are unmistakable. I am seized with raw panic. Akéla must be warned! I get onto a side street. I do not know how to ride a bicycle, but here I am suddenly "flying" over the pavement astride one. Though I have absolutely no recollection as to the mystery bicycle's origins, I reach the house, jump off, rush upstairs and breathlessly inform them of the enemy presence only blocks away. They manage to remain outwardly calm and to calm my anxiety as well, and they urge me to carefully retrace my steps. Somehow I get back to the château, on foot I think, the way I started out. All is quiet. The Nazis are gone... To this day I cannot understand or satisfactorily explain the bike incident, but it is most vividly present in my mind. Pol and I laughed about it subsequently. He didn't know either. It didn't really matter, after all; but unforgettable, nonetheless.

The main Catholic holidays are always extolled and dutifully observed, both religiously and to promote community (strictly our very own, of course) spirit. In my mind, the Christmas pageant stands out for the weeks of preparation and the feverish involvement. The living crèche was quite a tableau. Yours truly was a brown squirrel near the manger, with a long, stuffed stocking as a not-so-magnificent tail; I don't think that little critter figured in the original, but I was so proud to be in the picture at all. Songs and recitations, even special smells, and the very dark blue, almost black uniforms Maman Taquet and her staff had, somehow, managed to sew for each one of us: jackets and short pants, and capes. Garnished with our scouting neckerchiefs. I am wearing the outfit and carrying our pennant as we proudly (but cape less) "pass in review" in front of the Taquets and the Princess of Merode's retinue, Akéla smartly leading us.

Fishing in the Semois, catching little "goujons" with bent pins and string, makeshift poles. I kept some in a can on a window sill one summer. When I finally reopened it... Shudder! The smell was so horrendous it made me cordially hate fish for years thereafter, until my first bite of halibut at Bernstein's Fish Grotto on Powell Street in San Francisco.

And also splashing about in the Semois, in our underwear of course. There was also a water mill, with its deep black pond. Getting thrown in was very frightening and gave me a deep-seated fear of water. Took years for me to learn to stay afloat; not until Fort Hood, Texas, in the fifties, did I feel relatively at ease in it.

Occasionally the cubs all hike to the Abbaye d'Orval.

Paul A. Schwarzbart

This 900-year-old monastery is world-famous today for its artisanal trappist ale and cheese. It's only an 11 Km. trek, but for our little short legs, it's so very far away. Berets and black capes (or were they midnight blue?) We each had such an outfit. We really enjoy these very exciting day-outings, a welcome break in the routine, marching and singing, wonderful camaraderie. Until we tire and start losing our stamina. Until we start dying of thirst and hunger. Akéla encourages us, telling us wondrous stories. Cool water and sandwiches upon our arrival there. And a well-earned rest, around the countess' spring, "La Fontaine de Mathilde", where a twelfth-century legend tells of a magic trout that rose to the surface, holding the lady's lost wedding ring in its mouth. This aunt of Godfrey of Bouillon is said to have exclaimed in delight: «Why, this is truly a 'val d'or'!» Hence the name of «Orval», Golden Valley. The very modernistic church, the entire façade covered by an enormous Madonna and child. And inside, in the cool semi-darkness, the beautifully haunting voices of the monks raised in song and prayer. The old ruins, ever-present reminders of destructive fires, mark a distant past for us. Occasionally, Madame Taquet and the Major drive up and share our visit. And then the long, long trek back, and the waiting supper. And more tales. And sleep, marvelous and deep sleep. No falling asleep, no time for lonely sadness, just exhausted and immediate oblivion. On an initial return visit in the sixties, with Gail and Pol, what an incredibly short distance, 11 Km. by car! But the jambon d'Ardennes and the Orval beer were delicious indeed… A new titillation of the recall mechanism.

When we occasionally have scouting evenings on the old tennis grounds, campfire and all, we sing and play skits written by us. I dream of an heroic story, where I save my fellow cubs from the Germans but must sacrifice my life in the process. I never produce these skits, of course, for the war is not an acceptable topic. But I dream them, I dream them… Revenge, heroism, revenge.

At our reunions, people talk about being in therapy all these years. Why haven't I felt the need? Yet, as I think about these fantasies, perhaps I should have availed myself of these support groups, too.

These days, as I sat in the sanctuary during terrorist alerts, with sheriffs' cars in the parking lot, I have fantasized about terrorists appearing in the doorway. How would I react? Would I be heroic and help save Sharry and the others? Would I have to die to kill the killers? These are extremely difficult words to write, and not only because of the perspiration suddenly obscuring my view and flooding my palms.

I used to imagine, very vividly indeed, catching my dear father's torturers and skinning them alive as payback. Can monsters turn us into monsters, or is what I contemplated not monstrous in that context?

And yet, I do perceive myself as a gentle man.

One relatively newfound (1988 reunion) former fellow-cub leader, the erstwhile Charles Bergenboom (Charles Berkenbaum, subsequently a Brussels psychiatrist) defensively confesses to me his constant and deep jealousy of me in Jamoigne, because he perceived me as Akéla's favorite. Apparently there was a raging rivalry, but one of which only he seemed aware. Until he told me, I was even unaware of him! Can the past really be so tinted by the present? I made several efforts, even visited them in Waterloo. But no sign of life, no responses for many years now. Many I meet "for the first time", the years have obscured them, made them fade into a haze of forgetfulness. Others, very few, are crystal-clear and sharp. Two have remained close, Jacques and David (whom some, but not I, still call Daniel). One seemingly more than the other. We understand each other, and when we speak, it is open and warm, and time passed between visits is secondary at best. Selective memory is indeed a scalp-scratching puzzle! But distance, it seems, does not necessarily nor always make the heart grow fonder...

VI.

July 25, 1943, dawn. My second month of safety and relative tranquility. Suddenly, the unmistakable sound of German boots and armaments reverberating through the courtyard and up into our dormitories. We are ominously surrounded by the "entire" German army. In point of fact, it is but a platoon of the Feldgendarmerie, their field military police. Three trucks, personnel carriers, helmets, insignia, machine guns, enormous dogs, the loud guttural sounds of raw German, all the paraphernalia of terror. It's quite early, about five o'clock in the morning. Until then we had all been sound asleep. A favorite tactic, it seems, these "Blitz" intrusions at dawn. Two helmeted giants in rubberized rain gear, the now-familiar metal chain and crescent across the chest, machine guns hanging from the neck strap, have irrupted into my dormitory. Looking up at them, they appear much larger than life--and yet they clearly represent death. I am suddenly overcome by panic, I hold my breath, and my bladder summarily fails me once again. We are lying on very thin straw sleeping sacks serving as mattresses; the warm liquid engulfs my loins and immediately and forcefully oozes through the straw and drips "noisily" onto the stone floor. Sounds like timpani drumming to my frightened little ears! One of the soldiers hears the rhythmic sounds in the otherwise dead silence, looks under the cots, and straightens up laughing boisterously "This kid here just peed in his bed!" They both have a good chuckle and leave the room. Had either one of them simply thrown back the covers, the cat-and-mouse game would certainly have been summarily over! An eternity later, no more than a couple of hours perhaps, the "Boches" as we call them, pack up and depart--almost as quickly as they had appeared; but now they are triumphant; they have a prisoner in tow: Mouton (Comblain Gordon) had tried to evade them. The dogs smelled his still-warm bed and dragged him off the rooftops immediately. I have since heard that an anonymous letter had informed the Germans of the presence of a British aviator among the monitors. Pauvre Mouton! All I know is that they were obviously not looking for me, for I would have been so incredibly easily identified. Suddenly, quite unexpectedly, the war has come back to us, the intrusion hitting us full in the face. Our serenity, tentative though it may have been, is absolutely shattered. It takes us days to get over the shock. I know that morning, like so many others, has marked me deeply. Mornings indeed...

September 7 or 8, 1944. I am told now that there were massive German troop movements those days, but we all are ignorant of it at the time. I'm also totally ignorant of the Allies' landing, almost exactly three months before. The Taquets and some monitors, however, must know. We awaken to the unmistakable sound of heavy shell fire. Even we understand what we are hearing, for the explosions are in such close proximity. But why, what's going on? Not just unusual, a first indeed. We can see and hear two German tanks, the Wehrmachtskreuz insignia are unmistakable, near the bosquet. Their guns are firing repeatedly. Some time later on there is but one left, and it is ablaze. We all go outside, through the cour d'honneur. There is gunfire, bullets are whizzing about like supersonic bees, even mortar shells are exploding nearby. It's coming from and directed into the large wheat field beyond the château. We are standing about, mouths agape. Even the grown-ups are enthralled, and so we completely fail to take refuge inside, deep in the old cellars and subterranean passageways where there certainly would have been safety for all of us. After what seems a very long time, the sound of motors. And emerging from the central avenue, a column of small vehicles and foot soldiers, still firing into that field. Someone utters "They're Americans!" The Americans?

Why not Martians? Disbelief. Shock. They are all so tall, so clean-looking. One is firing what I now know to have been a .45 pistol, legs wide apart, one forearm used to support the unbelievably loud, kicking weapon. The vehicles, jeeps, have long, very long flexible poles on them. Fishing gear we think, for they must have heard about our river Semois and its fish population. They are, of course, mobile radio antennas. None of us has ever seen anything like it before. The battle lasts. I don't see any casualties, certainly none among us. An absolute miracle! And suddenly, as suddenly as it started for us, it is all over! And we are being hugged by tall young men, really not that much older than we, our cheeks tweaked. Hershey bars, chewing gum ("What's that?"), delectable (!) field rations, everything just so delicious. After gorging ourselves, we scrape the wax off the cardboard containers and improvise makeshift candles. Luxury! We make our way to the main road, outside the gates. Columns of G.I.s as far as the eye can see, moving steadily on either side of the winding roadway. Occasionally, a German soldier, hands clasped behind his head, being marched down the middle, a long knife held at his back by a local "maquisard", no longer the threatening and feared conqueror. Oh Joy! Vive la liberté! The euphoria is indescribable. Sheer pandemonium! Great events happen so simply, so quickly. We are free... Hurrah! The troops are encamped nearby, about 2 Km. down the road, at the village of Les Bulles; somehow we are allowed to visit them there and even spend time with them. All steadfast routine has quite simply evaporated, a happy and welcome breakdown. The young soldiers make us feel so welcome, though we do not speak each other's languages. They can't spoil us enough, it seems. We just love them all. We are so elated, so grateful, so relieved. But I don't talk about my being Jewish, I don't even mention it. Some of them undoubtedly are too, but it never really occurred to me just then. There is time enough. But I dream, every moment, of being reunited with my parents, my family. No doubt in my mind: it will, it must happen now. And we soon learn that Brussels is free too, and I go to see my Godmother, whom I can now openly address as "Marraine", and secure her permission to leave for the capital. And I bid adieu to the Home, the sisters, the monitors, my friends, and of course, the Taquets, Pol and

Laurette Georis, and dear Father Hardy. One of the sisters, I don't remember which one, gives me her large cross. «Adieu mon p'tit Paul, bonne chance! Le Seigneur te protège!» And I strike out into the unknown. It's October now. Oddly enough, I have absolutely <u>no</u> recollection of the journey from Jamoigne to Bruxelles, none whatsoever. Nor how long it takes. Hypnosis has been suggested, but to what purpose? But now I am in Brussels once again, walking the streets of Anderlecht in the direction of my home, and about a block away I see Mutti making her way toward me. And she also recognizes me from afar, God only knows how. A mother's heart! And time stands still for us. And we fly forward in unison into each other's arms, we hug, we kiss, we sob, and we laugh out loud! Movie-like. In my now broken German, I tell her how very "house sick" I am, how desperately I missed her. So terribly homesick indeed, but "home" always means "Mutti". And we say to each other, over and over and over, that now we can await Papa's return together... He will surely be coming "home" too! The horror is really over—isn't it? Isn't it?

VII.

That first Friday evening after being reunited, Mutti benshes (blesses) the candles to welcome the Sabbath. Her hands move over the two tiny flickering flames, up to her face and then covering it, in ritual fashion, just as I remember my grandmother doing. A sublimely beautiful first for me, in almost two years. And without further ado or transition, I go back, very naturally, ever so simply, to being the Jew I always was and never really stopped being. Mutti very intelligently poses no superfluous questions. As a matter of fact, she listens rather than questions, and at the time we don't actually discuss the years we were forcibly apart. For <u>now</u> we are together again. That's the important matter. Many long years later, in the US, she recalls those wonderful moments. And then, and only then, she at long last mentions that seeing the large cross hanging from my scout belt that day in 1944 was like being stabbed in the heart for her... She uttered nothing at the time, however, not even a sigh, but it did weigh heavily on her mind. How did she stifle the words that were choking her? What a great, great lady! I honestly don't know what happened to "my" cross subsequently. I still own the missal, inscribed by Pol Georis and for which he had painstakingly and lovingly fashioned a leather slipcase. At the Washington DC, reunion of 2003, one of the former hidden children tells of her father unkindly wrenching her beloved Christian religious symbols (her rosary and her missal, among others) out of her clenched hands and then forcing her to watch him thrust them into the flames. Agony! She still misses those objects which afforded her so much comfort during her many dark hours, she still longs for them... No closure for her. I, however, was spared that particular traumatic experience, though I cannot know whether it would have been as traumatic or as lasting for me. Thank you, again and again, dearest Mutti, thank you! Can I ever say it often enough? No!

And the excruciating waiting continues. At the earliest opportunity, we start making countless official inquiries. No news of any kind, however, absolutely nothing. As though Papa had never existed. Le silence de la mort. Numberless bulletin boards all over town, with little slips of paper: "Has anyone seen so-and-so, last heard from in... on...??" The Wailing Wall. Heartbreaking. Could it be that war is hardest on the survivors? The agony of waiting and searching is indescribable. So many false hopes, dashed. I see Papa in every stranger walking past on the street. My heart beating faster and faster, I always follow him, doubling my stride, but when I catch up to him and furtively glance over my shoulder, it is never he! We cry ourselves to sleep at night, Mutti and I, but there are also occasional tears of joy and hope.

Winter 1944. A very harsh winter indeed. The last major and desperate German counter-offensive in the Ardennes, not too far from where I spent two years in hiding. The great and infamous Battle of the Bulge. So many brave young Americans lay down their lives for us. We are terrified even in far-away Brussels. People even speak of mass suicides, were the Nazis to make it all the way back here. There are tales of horribly cruel reprisals against the inhabitants and entire villages suspected of helping the resistance and the Allies during and since the Liberation. And relentless and merciless V1 and later V2 attacks against London, though as many flying bombs have defective trajectories and fall on Brussels and its civilian population instead. Scores are killed daily. But Mutti has tired of the air raids and stubbornly refuses to seek shelter below, when the sirens go off, so shocking still. She's just had enough. No more cellar huddling, no more fear of being buried alive. During the occupation, on top of everything else she had also feared detection, of course: would there be another raffle; would someone turn her in, out of spite, for the reward money, or for no reason at all? But now, if we are marked for death, then we shall simply die. We are both resigned. However, she does not want us to live disfigured... So we do resort to covering our heads and faces to ward off the shattered glass. And live we do. Was her life cut short by these experiences? I fear so.

VIII.

May 1946.

We return from Jamoigne. Our immediate war is finally over. But is it really? Can it really be the truth?? Eventually Omama somehow contacts us, my sweet Grandmother Lea, Mutti's beloved mother.

She is alive in London, where she courageously survived the Blitz, but she is all alone there. No one else is with her. She alone had made it to safety. At the time it seems that some questions were almost avoided, and I therefore recollect no details about her rescue. Or the disappearance of the others. She finally crosses the Channel for a first visit. Seven very long years of separation. She speaks English now, of course, but not a word of French. My now-tentative German is suddenly all-important for us. A bissele Yiddish (just a bit), too. And we do indeed communicate, with love. Grandmotherly bliss... "I fought the Nazis too, you know. Throughout the entire war, I worked in a clothing factory, sewing uniforms for our gallant British troops." Utterly alone, all alone in a strange country, under incredible duress, she learned the language, the customs, made a well-earned place for herself, and proudly contributed to the war effort.   Years later, after emigrating to the US and making our home there, she and Mutti will study so hard and so assiduously to learn all they can about their adoptive country. Immediately after the obligatory five-year waiting period, all three of us take the tests together and obtain our coveted citizenship certificates. The judge compliments me for having two such wonderful ladies and reiterates how very happy and proud he is to welcome us into the fold as new citizens! Just imagine the pride we felt, indeed the feelings that washed over us at that moment! I do wonder whether it is still such a marvelously personal experience today for our new immigrants?

Like Mutti, what a great lady, Lea Schneider! Such dignity. She brings me a beautiful English leather briefcase, my very first, and in my eyes, an absolutely magnificent piece of craft. Apparently, however, there is no such thing as perfect contentment. One of my classmates, out of sheer jealousy I suppose, scores it with a sharp object during the short interval between two classes. Absolutely incensed, I hurl the blackboard-cleaning water pail at his head--just as Mr. Lefèbvre appears at the door. No discussion, no questions asked: we are summarily marched off to the principal's office. Both of us are severely punished, but no restitution is forthcoming.   That poor briefcase served me well for a long time; it bore its scars with a very stiff British upper lip...

Omama's first visit is far too short, but thoroughly enjoyed by all three of us.

We show her the city, we try to see everything together. I am so proud to walk arm in arm with my two beautiful and adored ladies, and I simply bask in their love.

All my recollections about my parents and family continually amaze and confound me, and indeed deepen my already-profound respect and admiration for all of them. If I am anything today, it is an ode to them, to what they were able to instill in me. There cannot be thanks enough, ever!

Early spring 1945. The grapevine speaks of a recent "returnee" from Buchenwald. That's a name that people readily recognize. Reminiscent of the Weimar Republic. So Mutti and I travel across Brussels by streetcar and on foot and expectantly ring his doorbell. A tall, gaunt man appears. We do not introduce ourselves, we say nothing, for she had warned me to be wary, but he suddenly turns and addresses me, almost in a whisper, very quietly: "You must be Fritz's son, Paul!" Almost as if in a dream. Mutti blanches, trembling. We had been repeatedly warned about people making up stories about missing individuals, out of sympathy or to take advantage of a horrible situation. No question in our minds in this case, however. For it is true that I do very much resemble my father, though I could never hope to be as handsome as he. Thus, if the man recognizes Papa in me, if he remembers my very name, he must indeed and truly know him. And he must have recently been with him. But the poor wretched man is terribly sorry, he hasn't seen Fritz for quite some time, has lost touch with him and has absolutely no idea of his present whereabouts. So close, and yet...

On the roller coaster once again: from the heights to the depths. We are utterly dejected, and we just drag ourselves home. And the waiting and hoping resumes. There is no statute of limitation on dreams.

Mutti now begins writing to Papa's sister Herta, the one living in the States with her husband Leopold and their two little children Lawrence Anthony and Joyce Alma. My uncle holds a PhD in psychology from the U. of Vienna, a disciple of Jung, but during and after the war they ran a chicken ranch in Petaluma, California. In due course, I learn—according to the Britannica of the forties—that the little town is considered the egg basket of the world. Remember The Egg and I, with Claudette Colbert? That was Petaluma! Mutti and I saw the film in a Brussels downtown theatre, with absolutely no idea as to its real venues. The Störs are happy to know that we survived and my aunt is still hopeful that her brother did too, somewhere, somehow. We correspond faithfully, Mutti in German, and I in French, and eventually their so-long-awaited affidavit will procure us the magic visas to reach the land of milk and honey, a journey begun in 1938, during another lifetime... The subsequent wait will last some three interminable years though: we shall not lay eyes on "the Great Lady Liberty" until the dawn of December 8, 1948. Oh, what a day! I am writing these stream-of-consciousness recollections some fifty-six years later.

IX.

Times are very hard during these months separating our liberation and the actual cessation of hostilities. In our correspondence with the Taquets, they suggest I return to the Home until the world settles down a bit and they offer my mother the job of "overseeing housekeeper". Shelter and safety from the flying bombs, and a token income. How could she not grab the offer? I also think Mutti thought I needed more of a transition. Who will ever know?

The more I reminisce and research, the more I am in awe of my mother's profound intelligence and compassion. Whenever I think there is no limit to my respect and admiration for her, the facts convince me that even that is still an understatement.

And so, from April 1945 to May 1946, I find myself back at the Château once more. When I left here months ago, I felt somehow quite sure I would never set eyes on the place or the region again. This time I occupy a small room with my mother. The kids who are left are the ones whose families have not yet been able to contact them, or perhaps never shall. Now Madame Taquet is definitely my godmother, and I therefore have the great privilege of attending the village school. A one-room schoolhouse. I clearly remember the teacher, Mr. Erniquin: he had to teach all the villagers (and me) in turn. Sadly, when I returned so many years later on a pilgrimage, he had already died. I should really have liked to thank him. I always have, and shall always appreciate my mentors.

At the village kermesse, their fair, it suddenly snows that month of May! It's the 13th, and the village is celebrating V.E. Day. I come down with a fever. The village doctor, Dr. Dion, diagnoses pleurisy and orders complete bed rest. That means that I remain in bed for almost six months, on a force-fed diet of eggs, bacon (lard!) and butter. Reading allowed for one hour daily, and only answering a call of nature allows me to get out of bed at all, albeit very briefly. Mutti, Mme Taquet and the sisters are unrelenting. Occasionally the door is left open to allow the sounds of the chapel to reach me. Lovely singing. Father Hardy does look in on me too, but I am essentially left to my thoughts. When the good doctor, finally (!), judges me well, I am so roly-poly that I have to exercise to regain my walking ability... But it seems that these old-fashioned treatments really do work. In 1948, when I was examined by the American doctors in Antwerp before obtaining that ever-elusive visa, they really put me through hell about the pleurisy. Why did we tell them, for there were no medical records? When they were finally unable to find any scarring or traces of the disease, they (reluctantly or grudgingly, I think) gave me a clean bill of health. I would be admitted to the United States after all. What a relief!

And here I sit at the keyboard, musing, some fifty-nine years later... And remembering. A very slow convalescence following a tough bout with pneumonia. What a strange coincidence indeed.

X.

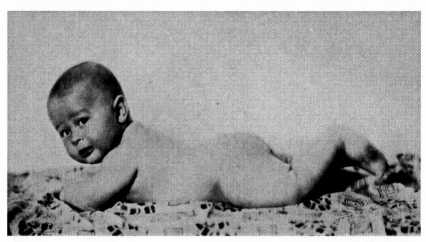

I burst onto the scene of this world and was named Paul Arthur on April 12th, 1933, after my paternal grandfather Arthur and my grandmother (his wife) Pauline; but I would always be "Pauli" and/ or "Paulinka" to my relatives and their close friends, the little love apple my parents wanted so, and my entire family's wish at long last come true. What an auspicious beginning, and what an awesome responsibility.

The situation in Vienna was already somewhat precarious, but not to me, of course. I fully and completely enjoyed the loving and nurturing attentions showered on me by all who knew me. We lived in the Dritten Bezirk (3rd district) of the city, across the street from a huge school. Our 3rd floor apartment was lovely, a long hall, spacious rooms, windows overlooking the street and the school. I particularly remember the impressive height of those windows and the wide cushions that protected the inner sill. Great seats for looking out onto the street below. I also remember how much the sight of our nation's flag, flying over the school on its façade, pleased me. I used to march enthusiastically to the sounds of music rising from the gramophone. There was always music. Leo Slezak... It instilled in me a great love, especially for opera, which has never waned. Music, like breathing, is a life-necessity.

My Papa Fritz (Friedrich) was ordinarily away at work, at the Internationale Transport Gesellschaft, where he occupied a position of trust and responsibility for many years.

Not for very much longer, however: the letter dismissing him for being a Jew will soon crush him.

Gegründet 1872.

INTERNATIONALE TRANSPORT-GESELLSCHAFT A. G.

Telegrammadresse: TRANSPORTAG
Telephon: U 26-5-50 Serie

Wien I, Hoher Markt 12
(Ankerhof)

Österr. Postsparkassen-Konto Nr. 83.617
Prager Postsparkassen-Konto Nr. 500.629

Frachtagenten der:
Erste Donau-Dampfschiffahrts-Gesellschaft

Rickmers Linie nach Ostasien

IHR ZEICHEN VOM: UNSER ZEICHEN: WIEN, am

Z E U G N I S .

Wir bestätigen hiemit, dass Herr Fritz S c h w a r z b a r t ,
geboren am 21. Oktober 1902 in Wien und dahin zuständig, vom
2. Jänner 1931 bis zum heutigen Tage in unseren Diensten gestan-
den ist. Herr Schwarzbart fand hauptsächlichst in unserer Export-
abteilung Verwendung und hat sich im Laufe der Jahre durch seinen
unermüdlichen Fleiss und seine Geschicklichkeit so umfangreiche
Kenntnisse erworben, dass er in seinem Wirkungskreis selbständig
arbeiten konnte. Wir waren mit den Leistungen des Herrn Schwarzbart in jeder Beziehung äusserst zufrieden und können ihm auch
hinsichtlich seiner charakterlichen Eigenschaften nur das beste
Zeugnis ausstellen.

Eingetretener Umstände halber mussten wir Herrn Schwarzbart
entlassen und begleiten ihn unsere besten Wünsche für sein ferne-
res Fortkommen.

Internationale Transport Gesellschaft A.G.

Wien, den 21. Juni 1938.

Mutti Sidi (Sara Ryfka) was professionally trained as a milliner/ modiste and made the most gorgeous hats for herself. She was always so beautiful, so elegant and refined. She took me everywhere with her. Ice cream in large cones at the neighborhood Kondittorei. I later learned that it was straight whipped cream dispensed to me, on my parents' strictest orders... I didn't actually taste ice cream as such until much, much later, and I do like it still. But I <u>really</u> enjoy whipped cream to this very day, but only the real heavy cream, no shaving mousse for my palate!

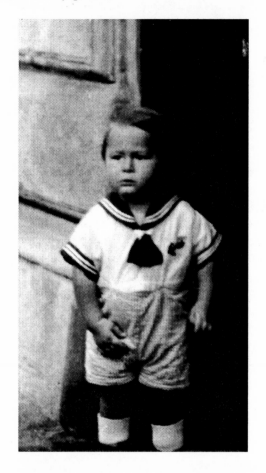

      My maternal grandmother Lea Schneider, Omama, lived but a few blocks away.

We spent a lot of time there. She was a seamstress, and I loved playing in her ground floor workroom and on the street in front of it, especially riding my tricycle. One day I was struck down by a bicycle and the toy cigarette holder I clenched between my teeth rammed my front teeth flat against my palate. The doctors fixed the problem, and I was soon nursed back to health. Must have taken years off my mother's life though. I also rode my tricycle in the park,

giving pretty (I'm told) little girls an occasional ride, and I also played with my huge hoop. I could actually fit into it. Small but feisty. Lots of photos of yours truly, often wearing a white sailor suit.

My father was a true shutter bug, and one of his prize possessions was his Voigtländer camera. I can still see him behind it, under the black cloth, focusing and composing. He had a great eye indeed, a born photographer, especially for portraiture. All ashes now.

The lady in the apartment next to ours must have been married to a hunter—or at least had a hunter or a taxidermist in her life. She used to invite me in, but I truly hated going there. The endless hallway was lined with stuffed trophies: birds of prey mounted in full attack mode, wings outspread, beaks open, and talons reaching out. Large birds still give me the willies, though I finally did approach a golden eagle in Alaska last summer without any ill effects; but Volta did not appear at all confrontational, though his stare was piercing and unforgiving. I wonder whether that lady in Vienna actually enjoyed frightening me, for my fear must have been rather evident to her... Come to think of it, the German Adler was a hundredfold more terrifying than those dead birds. Even the Austrian flag displayed the eagle(s), but quite stylized by comparison. I'll take Alaska anytime, however, and I'll never forget proud and beautiful Volta, the Magnificent. A national symbol of a very different ilk.

So, all things considered, I was a thoroughly happy kid. I felt truly loved and cherished, and in return I adored my parents. I looked forward to our visits to my father's mother and sisters, though they were rarely all there together.

My grandmother Paula presented me with my first Rucksack. Leather, of course. So proud. It was a long ride on the streetcar and a whole adventure for me. My entire family loved me, and I was always given lots of presents. I remember my excitement at my first (and only) leather soccer ball and the special "needle" with a wooden handle to thread the laces through after filling the bladder with air. Kept that for the longest time. Strange remembrances and souvenirs, because I never had a chance to actually play soccer with that particular ball.

Both my grandfathers had fallen "heroically!" for Austria: Arthur Schwarzbart in 1914 at the age of 39 and Hersch Wolf Schneider in 1915 at the age of 40. So of course I never really knew them, only from photographs and so many, oft repeated, family stories.

My paternal grandfather Arthur was dashingly handsome and sported a huge handlebar moustache. He was a gifted artist. My aunt Herta a few weeks ago gave me a box of the postcards he illustrated so beautifully and sent my grandmother Paula from the field. My maternal grandfather Hersch Wolf

was a tailor, as his surname implies. Grandmother Paula reared her four daughters with the help of my father, who, as the only male, very naturally assumed these heavy responsibilities. His sisters, my dear aunts Hilde, Ella (Gisella), Hansi (Johanna) and Herta, adored Fritz. It was mutual. My grandmother Lea reared my mother and her sister Rose alone, though my mother really took care of her younger sister most of the time; until some years later, when Lea married my grandfather's brother Israel, himself a widower, thus retaining the family name.

He too was a tailor, and my mother and her sister continued to call him "uncle" most affectionately throughout his life. Assuming full responsibility for one's brother's widow and orphaned children is another very compassionate and rather beautiful tradition of our people. Would we still be in existence without such humane traditions and continuity?

XI.

One morning in March of 1938 (I had not quite yet turned five), my parents awakened me rather early and carried me into the room facing the street. They raised me to the window, and I sat up on the thick cushions. As I looked across at the school, I immediately noticed that "my" beloved flag had been replaced by one I had never before laid eyes on, a huge red flag, with a huge white circle in the middle, and with an even huger and strangely symmetrical bizarre-looking black hooked cross (aptly named Hakenkreuz) in the center of that huge white circle. I did not yet know the swastika, but I became acquainted with what it represented soon enough. And I'll never forget the look on my parents' faces. There was despair, which of course I did not comprehend. They, however, did, only too well! But no one among us truly knew what was in the offing. How could we, how could anyone? There were throngs in the streets, loud and boisterous throngs. Noise and confusion, not at all the quiet neighborhood to which I was accustomed. So many little replicas of that large flag being waved about. Anschluss! Another word I would have to acquire and try to understand. But how could I? Later on that morning, when we went down to the street, my lifelong playmates pushed me away and told me, dirty little Jew, to go play in the gutter where I belonged! I knew I was a Jew, but I had never, ever before been accused of being dirty. Those cute white sailor suits, those ruffles, those little lacquered shoes...

My parents were so fastidious that I always, and only, made an absolutely immaculate appearance. So that appellation of "dirty" was totally incomprehensible to me. And to my dismay, I also realized that the adults, their parents, wore buttons in their lapels that closely resembled or duplicated the flag that now flew over the school. Others carried and waved little ones just like it. Austrian Nazis were overjoyed to have become Germans, and generally speaking, the Nazis were welcomed with open arms. But I had my dear Papa and Mutti, and I knew I was safe nonetheless. As long as they were close by, nothing bad could possibly happen to me. But it already had; my life had been turned upside down. Things would never, ever, be the same again. Not for anyone. Alas, I, we, knew not!

At some time, I had to have my tonsils and adenoids out. Because of the political situation, my parents arranged for the operation to take place in the surgeon's private offices. Papa took me there on the streetcar. I was a bit frightened, I think, but he was always so reassuring. I remember the mask, and having to count backwards: zehn, neun, acht, sieben... The sickeningly sweet smell of ether. Overpowering. Oblivion. Then the long ride home, bed rest, ice to suck, being spoiled so tenderly by Mutti and Papa. Convalescence. Love. What's so different? I can sense it, but without comprehending it.

November 1938. Kristallnacht. Burning synagogues, looted and destroyed businesses, street beatings and mass arrests. The situation goes from bad to worse, so much worse, and my parents make the very difficult decision to leave our homeland. We are to smuggle ourselves into "neutral" Belgium, and there to await our visas to emigrate to the United States. I can now trace the Schwarzbart family roots in Austria back to the 1700's, so emigration was not exactly a self-evident matter. The plan is to rejoin Papa's sister Herta, who, along with her husband Leopold (Poldi and much, much later, Leo), is now living in California. Papa is leaving two sisters behind, Hilde and Ella. Mutti must part from her own dear mother, already in her fifties. Almost the entire family remains behind, somehow. What is to become of them? Heart-wrenching goodbyes. The big unknown. These are indeed very strange, extraordinary times. But I am five years old, and none of these decisions is mine to make... Not even consulted!

Köln, Cologne. Even today the name still evokes "4711", Mutti, aromas, flowers, freshness, good grooming. Not a true reality representation! We are at a refugee hotel, filled with wretched creatures like ourselves. So many little children. Such a cacophony! Belgium is said to accept refugees, once they are physically on Belgian soil. However, the problem is getting there, crossing the German border undetected. Everyone around us here has a similar goal, getting out! There are local men ("coyotes" in current American slang) who make it their very lucrative business to smuggle people across, but they specialize in either men or women and their children. And so we must, for the first time, actually separate. Papa joins a group of men and leaves with them. Mutti and I do the same, but with other women and little ones. Night, snow, cold. After trudging through the snow for hours, we are detected by Belgian gendarmes and escorted back to the border. Summarily, but not unkindly. Rather very matter-of-factly. And we are back at the same hotel, once again. I suffer from an acute ear infection and am in sheer agony. Mutti gets some warm oil and gently pours a spoonful into the throbbing ear. Better. We must try again, find another "passeur". We are very short of money, but somehow, Mutti manages to pay again, and that night we are off with a new group. Mothers! A memorable rite of passage, literally. Mutti is carrying another woman's little child on her shoulders, and I have to run along, occasionally grabbing her hand or skirt, my little boots and I sinking deep into the snow. I am five years old, but I am now leaving childhood behind, forever. The brightness of the snow, the incredible glare, it's almost like daylight. Houses, gardens, countryside, dogs barking, voices. After a seeming eternity of trudging, our guide informs us that we are no longer on German soil, shows us the way ahead, and disappears. He has earned his fees. All at once we can once more see some Belgian border guards and their dogs, just ahead. Hence, they must also see us! Miracle of miracles, they do not apprehend us. Germany is left FAR behind, and for all intents and purposes, we are free again! And the rest disappears in the sometimes-merciful fog of time.

XII.

Bruxelles, Brussels at long last. Papa has been waiting for us, and we are oh! so happy once again. Reunited. Together. Safe.

First, we must seek residence permits, and we obtain them after registering at the Rue Georges Moreau police station. Fate! No premonition of any sort. To pay off our permits, Papa will be sent to a work camp for some six weeks. But first he is allowed to settle us in. He has found a tiny apartment Rue des Bassins, No. 1. Not too far from the Störs, only about a long block, on a tangent. Mutti borrows an iron, presumably from a neighbor, and there she is, on the bare floor, putting together some semblance of curtains. It's the law: occupied apartments must have their windows covered! No furniture, so we have to get a used bed and a table. Papa manages, somehow. I vividly remember Mutti and I cleansing the bed's spring, a wire lattice, where bedbugs, ugly little creatures gorged on our blood, would hide or nest right where the wires cross. I hold the spring up while Mutti runs the flame of a candle under the cross sections. The bugs pop and splatter some blood--ours. Ugh! None of us speaks French, as yet. And then Papa is really gone, and Mutti and I are on our own for some six weeks. How to subsist? Work permits are out of the question. Belgium is a tiny country, and its jobs are reserved for Belgians only. Mutti, like so many other women in our predicament, finds a well-to-do Jewish family. She is hired as cook and housekeeper. Rue des Vétérinaires, a few blocks away. But I'm alone from early morning until quite late; I have to occupy myself as best I can, roaming the tiny "flat" -- the two rooms separated by the landing. Such joy when Mutti comes home. Food, too! Occasionally, she leaves me at the Störs. There I am surrounded by activity, for the entire family is involved in manufacturing fur gloves and mittens. Fresh fur stinks! But there is always food and things to do. Even helping out sometimes. Warmth, both kinds. And that's also where I first saw colored celluloid-like cones in the dressing area, containing the women's discarded long hair. Why not just throw it into a waste basket? I found it bizarre even then. I do remember all of them quite fondly. I am the apple of Fritz's and Sidi's eyes, therefore the precious little darling for the rest of them too. And in the W.C. on their landing, furtively so as not to attract undue attention, I also experience my budding sexuality. Extraordinary! Several apparently bored young girls in the building, quite willing to encourage and guide, albeit tentatively, my clumsily ardent curiosity. My very first glimpses and definitely premature fondling of female genitalia, parted little mounds, smooth, rounded, rubbing softly against a miniature penis held up ever so expectantly. Precocious? I think not. Merely the extraordinary nature of our situation, though exploration has always existed as a mark of the curious young. Yet surprising, unforgettable and life-imprinting, most delicious ephemeral shivers, however fleeting the stolen moments. Were these moments ever, ever evoked by any of my playmates subsequently? The Jewish ones were certainly turned into plumes of smoke... Birkenau... 1,500,000!

Eventually, Papa does return from the (Belgian) forced labor camp. Regained happiness at long last! The joy of family life, the happiness of being reunited. We are indeed very close, and not just by virtue of our rather cramped quarters. Early morning breakfast, so that I can see Mutti before she leaves for work, and again late awakenings to see her come home. Family times, the very best of times. The rest of the day is spent with Papa, exploring Anderlecht and other parts of this magnificent capital and its parks. Long walks take us to the end of the Rue de Wavre, past Place de la Vaillance, to the very beautiful and expansive Parc Reine Astrid, named for the beloved young queen who died so tragically. Such treats, the whole excursion. Papa also teaches me to write, block letters at first, and I proudly copy the missives he composes for me to our family still (back home) in Vienna. He rewards me with a spoon of sweet butter accompanied by a bite of dark chocolate, delicious to this very day. The writing whets my appetite, and I can hardly wait to get into "real" school, but I have to reach my sixth birthday first. My wish comes true in 1939, and I meet my to-be-beloved teacher, Monsieur Campé, at the École Communale No. 9 of Anderlecht, a mere block from our house. Joy and anticipation!

Joseph Campé, my deeply beloved first teacher, grades one through three: 1939-1942. A wonderful man and great teacher, very strict, very fair. Taught me French and so much more, and I adored him. He really laid the stable and firm educational foundation that guides me, and he gave me the love for learning that still drives me today. I also clearly remember the little wooden rulers he made for each of us, 10 cm. long and marked individually. We each had a small wood-framed slate and a slate stylus, with the obligatory round (pock-marked by rust) metal box containing a damp sponge; the slate was blank on one side but had sets of 3 lines on the opposite one, lines strategically placed to help us learn script--which we painstakingly did. I progressed so quickly under his tutelage that I soon rose to the top of the class. He would always compliment me and hold me up to the other boys as an example of what could be achieved with earnest application "Look at our little Austrian. Follow his example. Don't be so lazy!" So during recess the other boys would beat me up as payback. Ouch! They also called me "l'Autrechien" the other dog, instead of "l'Autrichien", the Austrian. One single letter change is all it took--great scrabble move. Kids are cruel in their cleverness. I don't believe Mr. Campé ever knew about the beatings he earned me. I'm no snitch, but Papa exhorted and taught me to defend myself. When I mustered the know-how and courage to start fighting back, returning almost as much as I was receiving, the bullies stopped their attacks. Small, but feisty, that is I... No question in my mind at all: self-defense is one's absolute innate responsibility!

We were singing one day, and I must have really hit a clinker, for he suddenly thundered "Schwarzbart! ne chante pas!" "Schwarzbart, (we were always called by our surnames,) don't sing!" I've been somewhat reticent about singing in public ever since, though I'm getting better. Self-consciousness appears to be lessened by age. Thus he was probably solely responsible for nipping a most promising operatic career in the bud... I think that was his only negative utterance to me, ever, but I shall always remember it vividly.

On his way to school every single day following Papa's deportation for internment, Mr. Campé would drop off a little paper and string-wrapped parcel for me. And so when I came downstairs and passed her open door, Madame Yvonne would hand it to me and say "From Mr. Campé!" It was always a sandwich. I can still smell the eggs, hard-boiled or scrambled! He simply wanted to make sure I had something to eat. Essentially a stranger, "just" my teacher... But not a stranger at all: a true Mensch, an exemplary human being who unobtrusively practiced what he so ably preached!

À propos of smells, I still have the aroma of the daily soup in my nostrils. Every boy had an enameled cup (mine was missing a lot of its enamel in places, black spots), and at noon our teacher served us some kind of warm soup. It was watery, flat, and absolutely delicious! I ate a lot of watery veggies those years, and I'm grateful that someone cared enough about the children to provide that food, sparse though it may have been. At home, Mutti would also prepare rutabagas, potato peelings, whatever she was able to glean; if I never have to look another rutabaga in the face, it's OK by me! Helped to keep us alive, however.

Madame Campé, Julia, was a milliner like Mutti and owned a lovely women's hat shop on the Chaussée de Mons. She was a charming, warm-hearted lady.

In 1942, when we Jews were forbidden to attend school, a terrible blow within our culture, which prizes education so highly, Joseph Campé retired from teaching. "If I cannot teach everyone, I shan't teach anyone." It could have cost him his life; the Nazis didn't accept that kind of defiant resistance, but miraculously he survived the war. Wouldn't talk much about it, though.

After Mutti and I left for the US in 1948, we corresponded assiduously with the Campés. Since they wanted me to avoid all artificial formality with them, they suggested I address them as "Parrain" and "Marraine", meaning Godfather and Godmother respectively. How deliciously kind and warmhearted of them. They never failed to encourage me and even sent me the Larousse Universel and later a subscription to "Historia", a monthly French historical review. Sadly, I never saw them again. When I was at long last able to visit Brussels in 1966, I rushed to their Anderlecht address, 56 rue Lieutenant Liedel, but was greeted at the door by a stranger who told me that both Joseph and Julia had died since our last exchanges. I visited their graves at the local cemetery and paid my sad and tearful respects. I was truly devastated, and I'll never forget these two kind and generous beings. They have indeed earned a place of honor within my family.

Number 1, rue des Bassins, a haven to us for some ten years, off and on for me. A four-story corner building, with its other façade opening onto rue Émile Carpentier. The first adjoining downstairs shop sells coal and vegetables. It's more like a garage-hole-in-the-wall than anything else, but that's where, whenever we are able, we buy fuel and veggies, mostly potato peelings and rutabaga turnips. Before the war, when my parents would call me "Pauli", the woman who ran the shop and obviously couldn't understand the relationship to "Paul" always addressed me as "Fauli". Odd and unforgettable. The ground floor corner itself is a café, owned and run by Madame Yvonne and her paramour, "Monsieur". Her daughter is a "pute", a prostitute. Everyone knows. During the occupation she made enough money to open her own place right after the libération. We had to visit her there once, but we talked outside her establishment, on the sidewalk... A very amiable young woman. Mme Yvonne has a loge to the left of the house entrance, with only a small passage separating her from her café. She actually lives on the first floor, in what is said to be a spacious apartment. Each other floor has two dwellings. Ours is on the third floor, but we don't have a full apartment. As we come up the stairs to the landing, our tiny, tiny little kitchen is on the left. To the right of the landing is another door, our all-purpose bedroom. Papa had installed hasps on the bedroom door, and so we have a padlock for it. Both rooms have a coal stove, cooking in the kitchen, heating in the other room. The diminutive kitchen was always warmer, of course. Schlepping coal up three flights couldn't have been easy for Papa or Mutti--or paying for it, either. In the left corner is another door. Inside, a sink, for water, and a closed cubicle: the W.C. Down a dark corridor at a right angle to that door is the second apartment, a real one, whose windows open onto both streets. All through the war another "pute" occupies those rooms. And a thriving business it is, too, for that lady of the night and day! Since the walls are very thin indeed, Mutti often covers my ears at night so I won't get too swift and colorful an education. I hear most of the goings on though. Unfortunately, much of it goes literally way over my head! Her clientèle usually arrives in uniform, from the various German ones to the collaborators' stark black. Their minds are obviously on different matters, for they never bother us. Every time Mutti meets one of these men on the stairs, either coming or going, she is afraid for her life. But she tells me, after the liberation, that they are usually quite civil to her. Some Germans, she says, even address her with the most courteous greeting of "Gnädige Frau" meaning "Lady full of grace and mercy", though after 1942 they can plainly see she is wearing the Yellow Star. "Gnädige Frau" to a Jewess?! Go figure...

From our kitchen window we can see across the street and to the corner, the droguerie and the small Delhez grocery; and from the bedroom we have a much fuller view, all the way up rue Éloy, past the school. At the corner, directly across from my school, stands No. 89, where live the Störs and so many other families we know. The Nazis will subsequently pull up with their trucks and empty the entire dwelling of all its occupants--none of whom will ever return. Hell does not spew out its victims! Mutti and I watch from our window, impotent and distraught. Are we to be next? The infamous and dreaded "rafles" (round-ups) do indeed empty two more buildings across the street and the one adjacent to ours. But our house, number 1, rue des Bassins, is spared. Could it possibly be because of the oldest profession being plied here, frequented almost exclusively by the occupying rulers and their minions? Is the house therefore "off limits"? Perhaps we owe our lives to our neighbor. What is very clear, however, is that the Gestapo knows exactly who and where we are; they hold all the police files and we are duly registered. No question at all about that. I often wondered what became of that neighbor lady, for when I returned in 1944, she was gone without a trace. And people in the neighborhood claimed to have no knowledge of her at all. The righteous hypocrites who took charge ostensibly didn't want to forgive the girls who "slept" with the enemy in the occupied countries. Too many embarrassing revelations were possible and probable. Many a political career was thus grounded in murder to obfuscate the truth. Some of these foul creatures became police officials, government ministers and even presidents! But those sad women on the other hand, almost the tiniest fish in the pond, indeed made ready and easy scapegoats. And so they paid, some with their scalps, others with their very lives. The French have an apt term: "écoeurant"--makes you want to vomit! Madame Yvonne's daughter escapes the net and continues plying her lucrative trade. Let me confess here and now that at the time I was of that very same mind: punish everything that moves and looks guilty--get revenge! I did not yet know of, or even suspect, my poor father's horrible death, but I did know I wanted blood. Would blood at long last give me closure? But whose...? And is closure indeed a feasible reality for any of us?

In Brussels every citizen is responsible for the city's spic-and-span cleanliness and appearance... Hence all the houses are equipped with façade faucets near the front entrance, and the owners are enjoined to keep their sidewalks pristine, all year long. What a straightforward and responsible idea. Not to mention the obvious safety factor: no debris, no ice, no snow, no slush, no hazards! Radical. And fines, I am told, are duly levied for any infractions. And so Mutti does indeed scrub and keep the sidewalk in front of the Exsteen home clean, no matter the season. The uncommonly hard work, the starvation diet, the unspeakable stress, could all that be at the root of the rheumatoid arthritis that is to plague her mercilessly and so cruelly for years and ultimately cause her untimely death? No doubt in my mind!

Papa uses every spare moment to study English, usually at the kitchen table, near the window for better light. "By the time we reach the U.S., I must know the language well." Profound pride and self-awareness of the would-be immigrant, ready to make a worthwhile contribution to the country that adopts him. It behooves the newcomer, nay it is his or her absolute and primary responsibility, to know or learn the tongue and thus become productively integrated into the new society. Never to be a burden, never ever a parasite, au contraire. Another priceless and ever-guiding life-lesson he instills in me, deeply and indelibly. I know he has a tutor, probably only a slightly more advanced acquaintance, but that's all. There are several shiny black notebooks, three I think. German texts and English translations. He is so fastidious in his approach, so incredibly neat. Tight, evenly formed calligraphy. He writes in indelible pencil, line after line; the writing, in my mind's eye, sometimes appears ink-like. Purplish, perhaps... A few corrections, a few complimentary evaluations from his coach. Again, I learn so much from him. A great and loving teacher!

Today, I have absolutely no patience for the myriads of people who live here without bothering to learn English. Given the incredible opportunities and freedoms here, I cannot find it in me to excuse this blatant shortcoming. Of course, this is fostered even further by translating the very voting ballots... We seem to bend over backwards, until we snap our own backs. Dear God! No common sense!

Papa's weekly or bimonthly electric train journeys to Antwerp, to make tireless and oft-repeated inquiries at the American Consulate. He always returns deeply disappointed, though never hopeless. How incredibly discouraging this must be to him, to them both. But he is not to know that his efforts are futile. FDR's directives are both clear and lethal for Jews (as we now finally understand, utterly heartbroken!), and my father is never to obtain the coveted visas to enter the land of milk and honey. No, he is to die in the annihilation camps instead. And Mutti is destined to be a widow, and I, fatherless, and my sons, never to enjoy the warm embrace of their wonderful grandparents... Politicians who are just that, first and foremost, ostensibly and willingly shed their humanity! And oh so sadly, others have to pay the price. And now, just recently, Harry S. Truman's diaries come to light too. Clay feet indeed...

Our daily walks invariably take us to the little neighborhood park, a block away, halfway between home and the big bridge over the canal, and I enviously watch many neighborhood kids going down the entrance incline on their "beautiful" trottinettes, their scooters. I want one so, but I understand, I think, that it cannot be. Our "normal" lives aren't truly normal. Nothing has been normal for us since last year. Occasionally, a boy lets me make the ride down on his prized toy. Fantastic. It's barely a grade, but I remember it as a very steep hill.

Papa takes me to my very first movie: Disney's <u>Snow White</u>. It is playing near the city hall, in a small Catholic school. Another strange coincidence, but that actually never occurred to me until this very moment, as I write. Since I don't understand English and cannot read the French subtitles (I think they were there), I depend completely on the constant and steady narration Papa whispers to me throughout the duration of the film. I am enthralled and simply love the seven dwarfs and all the wonderful animals Disney created so artfully. But it is the only movie I ever experience with my father, and that alone makes it extraordinary. I recently bought the DVD immediately upon its release, but we have yet to watch it.

There is a toy shop window, a very narrow one. It's Chaussée de Wavre, I think. Or perhaps Rue Émile Carpentier, just around the corner. Papa and I walk by, daily, and we always stop. There is a mounted Napoleonic hussar, the horse rearing, and the officer, resplendent in his uniform, brandishes his gleaming curved sword. He is truly magnificent, and I want him so. I know he's too expensive, but every time Papa returns home, I somehow expect him to be bringing me that wondrous horseman. It never happens, of course. In spite of the abnormal situation, I still have a little boy's normal longings. I think I understand though, because I truly know how much my dear parents love me. If they could, they would hand me the moon--wrapped in a bow.

Papa routinely takes me to school in the morning and always picks me up in the afternoon. I walk so proudly, hand in hand with him, and we converse. When school closes, I know he's waiting for me at the courtyard gate, smiling. It makes my heart beat faster, and I so look forward to seeing him again. He is usually the only father there, for most of the others are at work; so the majority of kids are all picked up by their mothers. I was recently told, repeatedly, that people in the neighborhood remember the two of us, together. Much later in life, I ordinarily pick up our sons from school, too. Regularly the only father among all the mothers. Full circle... Gail often had the morning Schlepp.

In 1946, subsequent to our return to Bruxelles from my second stay in Jamoigne, I finish my last year of elementary school at the École Communale No. 9 in Anderlecht, under the guidance of M. Jules Haché, another memorable teacher. I've been so very lucky in that regard. Next will be Mr. Y. Lefèbvre, at the École Moyenne d'Anderlecht I still display my school cap, bearing 3 stars, in my study...

Memorable years at the École Moyenne. Wonderful teachers, wise administrators (!) and a top-notch student body. Essentially we were all there to work very hard and succeed accordingly. Clear and simple, isn't it? Very long walks to and from, and home for lunch, of course.

Mutti was at work, employed by a large sewing concern, a kind of sweat shop really, where she did fine hand finishing. She had "blessed" hands. She always worked so incredibly hard, never hesitated. So she had to pay for me to take my noon meals at the café. Mme Yvonne presided. My two luncheon companions were always Mademoiselle Diane (Cnudde) and Monsieur Fernand (Kuhn), older lovers for whom this was their daily assignation. The raw plot of a nineteenth-century French novel, really. We became great friends, in spite of my youth. They even gave me my very first copy of Alexandre Dumas Fils's La Dame aux camélias. Much later, when I first heard Verdi's La Traviata, I was delighted to recognize its familiar plot. I was an absolutely avid reader, and the local librarians knew me well. All the French classics and Alexandre Dumas, Shakespeare (whom I love to this day), even James Fenimore Cooper, Curwood, Dickens, Sir Walter Scott. I just couldn't get enough, it seems. Mr.

Lefèbvre assigned voluminous outside reading and the ensuing critical book reports, at which I seemed to excel. Homework, reading, and movies--whenever Mutti could, or could not, afford it. She just loved to please me, but I wonder how she managed it. All the current French films plus Disney, Lassie, Errol Flynn, Nelson Eddy and Jeannette McDonald... Escapism? Of course! And arm-in-arm over the cobblestones, so very close, through the dark and empty streets, home. Occasionally a "cornet" of hot fries, from the "roulotte" of a street vendor just closing for the night.

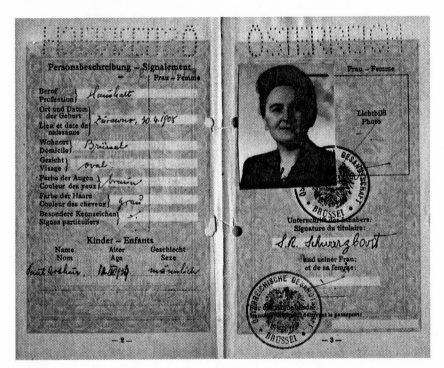

INDICATIONS IMPORTANTES

Le titulaire de ce permis doit le présenter à toute réquisition régulière.

Ce permis n'est valable que pour l'emploi (catégorie professionnelle), et pour la localité qui y sont indiques.

En cas de perte, de destruction ou de détérioration du permis, son remplacement doit être demandé par l'intermédiaire de l'Administration communale qui l'a délivré.

La délivrance du duplicata donne lieu à perception des mêmes droit et taxe que celle du permis original.

Toute infraction expose à des poursuites judiciaires et peut entrainer l'éloignement du Royaume.

BELANGRIJKE AANWIJZINGEN

De titularis van deze vergunning dient haar op ieder regelmatig gedaan verzoek te vertoonen.

Deze vergunning geldt enkel voor de betrekking (beroepscategorie) en de plaats erin aangeduid.

In geval van verlies, vernietiging of beschadiging van de vergunning dient de vervanging aangevraagd door bemiddeling van het Gemeentebestuur, door hetwelk zij werd afgeleverd.

De aflevering van het duplicaat geeft aanleiding tot de inning van dezelfde rechten en taxen als voor de origineele vergunning.

Elke inbreuk stelt bloot aan gerechtelijke vervolgingen en kan de uitzetting uit het Rijk tot gevolg hebben.

ROYAUME DE BELGIQUE
KONINKRIJK BELGIE

MINISTERE DU TRAVAIL
ET DE LA PREVOYANCE SOCIALE
MINISTERIE
VAN ARBEID EN SOCIALE VOORZORG

PERMIS DE TRAVAIL

ARBEIDSVERGUNNING

Avis important

Sans préjudice des dispositions qui régissent les passeports, le présent permis n'est valable qu'accompagné d'une pièce d'identité munie d'une photographie estampillée.

Toute altération du permis entraîne des poursuites judiciaires

Belangrijk bericht

Onverminderd de bepalingen welke de reispassen beheerschen, is deze arbeidsvergunning enkel geldig indien zij vergezeld is van een identiteitsstuk voorzien van een gestempelde photo

Elke alteratie aan de vergunning berokkent gerechtelijke vervolging.

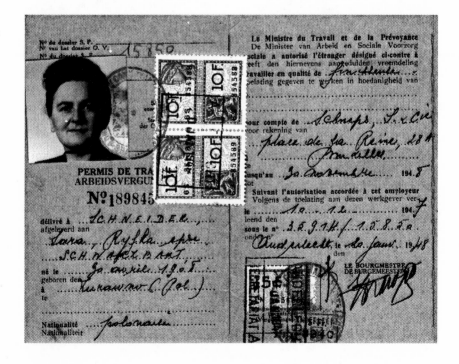

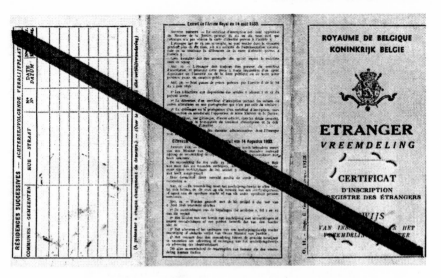

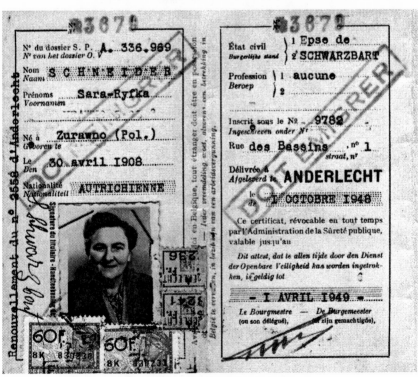

After the war, textbooks were non-existent or extremely scarce. So Mutti had to buy me my Latin book, which we finally found at a downtown bookstore on the chic Rue Neuve. An entire shopping adventure. Dressed up for it, of course, including hat and gloves; I wore my school cap proudly, way back, the visor flat on the top of my head. And on the Rue Neuve, replete with beautiful stores and shops, we taste our first milk shake. The fancy pastry shop offers three flavors ("parfums" in French): vanilla, of course, rich chocolate and real strawberries. The very height of luxury and decadence, perhaps. Again, just how did Mutti manage it? As for the other subjects, we relied on our lecture notes; they were copious and had to be faithful to the letter. Mr. Lefèbvre checked every page rigorously, even the punctuation. So much depended on our note-taking, that I recopied them all laboriously at night, reading them out-loud as I wrote. This daily practice served as study time too, and I therefore learned many facts by sheer rote. This almost got me into trouble once. After a particularly difficult history final examination, as a classmate and I (I think it was Gerlach or perhaps Huybrechts) were walking home on the Chaussée de Mons, we heard our names being called loudly behind us, and we were summoned back to school, pronto! The teacher had perused our papers and we were summarily accused of cheating! Luckily for us, we had not been seated near one another. We were both such fastidious note takers that our answers were literally identical. But as we were also both able to recite them to the teacher upon demand, the matter was simply dropped. I suppose that had this happened in the US, we would have been entitled to an apology. Not there, however!

I was subsequently awarded some end-of-the-year prizes for my achievements, particularly in French. Wonderful books! I don't suffer from false modesty, so I can happily say that it happened year after year. I truly earned these prizes, and Mutti had again reason to be proud. And so did Mr. Lefèbvre, I recall distinctly. Perhaps that is where I learned to be so very proud of my own students' successes, much later. But I never failed to thank my teachers, understanding full well where gratitude was due... Happily for me, I was able to visit some of them on many occasions, and I remain pleased with that fact.

The Chaussée de Mons also brings back the memory of the "bains-douches" which Mutti and I were very occasionally able to visit. We could not afford two separate baths, of course, so we paid for only one and took turns in the same tub of soapy water, one after the other, quickly because of the time limitation... A warm bath, what a luxurious delight nonetheless. Aromas and sensations.

So many movies. Escapism, no doubt. And so exciting, challenging, entertaining, fondly remembered to this day. How did Mutti manage the extra expense? And my introduction to the world of opera, at the prestigious Théâtre de la Monnaie: <u>Cavalleria Rusticana</u> and <u>Pagliacci</u>, of course. I was hooked—and am to this day. She was so incredibly sensitive to the needs she knew I had, though perhaps I was not that aware. What would have become of me, what would I have become, had it not been for the extraordinary care my beloved parents bestowed upon me so lavishly and so selflessly?

Of course I also vividly remember carrying some of Papa's things downstairs, to the lady living below us, who would occasionally purchase them for her husband. A pittance, to be sure, but a help to both parties. Mutti just couldn't do it, I assume, for it was me she sent down to propose a shirt, a pair of trousers, whatever... And so she made ends meet, somehow. Extraordinary, to be sure.

XIII.

Paris. Winter. Rue Lepic. That distant relative (I have no recollection whatever, as to who this man was) who accompanies us to the train station as we prepare to leave for Le Havre to board the ship waiting to transport us to the land of milk and honey. It is bitter cold on the train, and he returns from the WC holding his own long johns, which he gives me with the assurance that they are perfectly clean and exhorts me to slip them on immediately. Another Mensch.

Le Havre. The ship to paradise. Ironically, there is a dockers' strike, and our boarding of the S/S <u>Ronda</u> is delayed by several days. We have to survive on what little money we have. I remember cafés that balk at our request to share a plate... Another example of Mutti's determination and courage. And we do indeed survive the delay, somehow.

XIV.

1988. Thunderstruck! A completely unexpected, and at first bizarre, letter arrives. Indeed a tribute to the USPS's determination to "deliver"—for the given address was anything but straightforward. The return address reads "L'Amicale des Anciens de Jamoigne." Yes, indeed, I see myself as a former attendee of Jamoigne, but until now I am totally unaware of any such group's existence. Very strange indeed. It is a formal invitation to a reunion of all the Jewish boys who attended the school. What, a reunion of me with me? No. As I read on with utter disbelief, the long lists of names, all double, names I recognize on one side, names I don't recognize on the other. All except one: Paul Exsteen/Paul Schwarzbart! And it slowly dawns on me, I was not the lone Jew in hiding there after all! There were over sixty of us, hidden among the one hundred twenty-five... After the initial shock, I remain dumbfounded. Gail and the boys are, too. Wow! In all our contacts and correspondence, neither my Godmother nor my Godfather had ever revealed this absolutely monumental truth to me. Had they assumed I knew? The enormity of the deception perpetrated on the barbarians leaves me speechless. But I cannot attend this projected reunion, for I shan't know or recognize anyone after so many years apart, I simply cannot see myself doing it. Gail and the boys reason with me, I'd always regret not going, I must go! God love them, they prevail! And so I make plans to go. I contact philanthropic organizations, but the great majority turn me down. It seems that assistance to individuals, no matter how worthwhile the undertaking, is not forthcoming. A few students and friends, very few, offer me tangible help and I finally have my ticket for the journey into the unknown. I am also contacted by KRON TV News, an NBC affiliate, requesting permission for one of their crews to accompany me to the reunion they somehow heard about. They are indeed a news agency. It's a public event, after all, so come ahead; it's certainly not up to me to grant or withhold permission. Many conversations. Clearly, I have no idea I am about to become the central figure of my own documentary film!

At the airport I finally meet Ken Swartz, accompanied by his charming wife Anne. And the huge Betamax camera, which Ken does not let out of his sight for a moment. Their baggage load is enormous; they explain that it's mostly equipment: a trunk full of 20-minute Beta tapes, playback machines and monitors, microphones, transmitters, receivers, and of course his all-important tripod. Wow.... definitely a first for me, and I'm wide-eyed and duly impressed.

A long and stuffy trip. Much anticipation, many misgivings. And then, Brussels. All the baggage is accounted for, except the famous tripod. How can they misplace such a huge black cylinder? We make it to the hotel and call equipment rental agencies all over the city. It's Saturday, which doesn't help. Ken needs that particular tripod model. In vain. We decide to go out for a bite. I follow my nose and lead us to a small neighborhood seafood restaurant. Delightful reception. We enjoy the most delicious lobster bisque any of us has ever had the pleasure of tasting. So memorably delicious, that it's still with me after all these years. Following that scrumptious meal we make our way back to the hotel. And there, facing us in the lobby, stands the big black cylinder containing the tripod, just waiting for us. Hurrah for the airline! Ken is very pleased. Sharing his relief, so are the rest of us.

Anderlecht. I can hardly wait to show Ken and Anne where we used to live. So here we are, standing in front of the building at number 1, rue des Bassins, looking up at the third floor windows. "Our" windows. The café is gone, it is now a fruit and vegetable shop. Looks foreign and somewhat exotic. The entrance to the house is the same. I am just standing there, not moving, as I have previously, the few times I have returned. Just another pilgrimage, I guess. But this time is quite different: Ken urges me on, literally pushes me in. "Go! What do you fear?" We slowly ascend the stairs. Third floor, not a soul. Both doors are unlocked, even slightly ajar. The kitchen is smaller than my memory of it, but there is a sink now, with the water conduit, copper tubing, on the surface of the wall. Not a professional plumbing job, I find myself remarking to myself. I slowly push the bedroom door open, revealing an almost empty room. Unoccupied, at least at present. A few boxes, almost like a storage space. There is a door in the wall adjoining the other apartment, the infamous one, but one I don't remember existing. Perhaps it was hidden by our wardrobe. I'm overwhelmed. It's all so tiny, so wretched. And yet we were a family here. A wonderful, cohesive and loving family. In the stairway, I make the comment to Ken, who is filming all the while, relentlessly: "You sure don't need much to be happy. Just love!" We make our way back down, where we are met by a small burly man. Friendly and curious. He's a Turk, the owner now. I try to tell him my family and I used to live there, so many years ago. Not much of a dent, and clearly not just a language barrier. Absolutely no point of reference or commonality. "Did you see the water connection? I put that in myself!" Very proud of the accomplishment. Doubtless, my last visit to the building. Enough suffices.

We continue touring the old neighborhood. The Exsteens' house is gone, replaced by new construction. How ugly, I muse. The factory has disappeared too.

In its place there is a huge stark stone-and-chains memorial to the Jews deported from Belgium. It's enclosed and locked. Adjacent to it, a tiny memorial to the resistance. Little children playing on the walls, running and laughing. North Africans, it seems. I talk to them. They have not an inkling of what this is. Though plainly marked in French, in Flemish and in Hebrew, no one has bothered to explain to them. "It's a park, Monsieur, is it not? " "Yes, indeed, a sort of park!" 89, rue Éloy, right across the street. And diagonally across, my old school. Looks the same, just a bit smaller, somehow. We push the huge door open on its creaky hinges. No one to greet us, to stop us, to question us. The enormous hall stands empty. The classrooms are there, behind closed doors. We make our way to the huge courtyard in back, where I played during recess, now literally so tiny, so empty. The past rushes at me, I see myself, I see Papa bringing me there, then waiting for me. I see Mr. Campé. I remember the beatings, then the fights, then the playtime. I see Mr. Haché. And the Flemish-speaking substitute who punched me in the nose once, making me bleed profusely; the fact that it happened, more frightening than the action itself. I never told anyone except Mutti about that incident before. The school still smells of learning. Definitely a good place, a haven. Not a soul meets us, there is no one outside the classrooms, no one roaming the hall. Of course not, school is in session... Ken's camera whirs on, relentlessly.

The old police station is still there too. Grimy. Black. Abandoned. Dismal. Wretched. Disgusting. I am completely lost in my thoughts, my mind's eye revisits the 10th of May, 1940. A bitter moment of communion with that day, so long ago. Silent tears. A last goodbye, perhaps. To that sorry site, certainly. Ken, too, is very quiet.

The Amicale is on its way to Jamoigne, to make the pilgrimage and affix the memorial plaque on the château's courtyard wall.

En 1943 et 1944 dans ce Château,
83 enfants juifs accueillis et protégés,
furent soustraits aux plans d'extermination
de l'Allemagne nazie.

Témoignage d'infinie reconnaissance
cette plaque rappelle
le dévouement et le courage
des membres du Comité Organisateur,
de la Direction et du Personnel
du Home Reine Elisabeth,
qui ont sauvé ces enfants,
au péril de leur vie.

Several bus loads. Georges (Jo) and Jean-Pierre Exsteen accompany me. What a day! Reminiscences, new acquaintances, stories, embraces, tears, handshakes, raw emotion. During a break, over a cool drink, Andrée Geulen-Herscovici tells me "You don't know who took you into hiding? It wasn't I, that's for sure." I'm aware of this, it was a man, after all! "You must consult the notebooks of the CDJ." "What notebooks? Whose? Where?" "At the Ministry of Health!" Andrée advises me, exhorts me to call without delay. She's very solicitous. A real Mensch. We're to become fast friends.

The reunion and official ceremonies. Unforgettable. The Consul Général of Israel reads citations and awards medals to so many monitors.

Righteous Gentiles, all. Parrain and Marraine are, of course, recipients too.

Maman Taquet is almost blind, but she can still "see" her boys with her hands. If required to, she would do it all over again, she says, smiling. Belgian flags. La Brabançonne.

And then a huge luncheon in the church hall, in the village. Breaking bread together is an absolute must. So many monitors are in attendance here, even Mouton, whom we thought dead after the Boches led him away, that fateful morning! He survived prisons and camps and was liberated by the Russians in the spring of 1945. They all suddenly don't seem so much older! Time has brought us even closer together, in so many different ways... More songs. Speeches. Standing together on the stage. And I introduce my two "brothers", finding out that the others picked their pseudonyms out of thin air--whereas I had a "real" family. Goodbyes. Promises to keep in touch, to remain close...

I never knew of the Taquets' very special plans for me, nor were they ever revealed to me directly. It wasn't until I saw Marie's filmed interview by Ken Swartz, that I finally realized they had wanted to adopt the little prince, as she said she and Émile called me in private. When I was happily reunited with my mother, these plans dissolved. What incredible human beings, those two.

119

The next day, upon my return to Brussels, I do contact the Ministry of Health. There are no appointments available in the very near future. "But I'm an American, just passing through. I'm leaving for home soon, and I must consult the four notebooks. I must find the entries pertaining to me, to my past as a child in hiding." "Oh, you're leaving for the US; in that case, do come by tomorrow!" Almost unbelievable kindness and understanding. I am so profoundly grateful. And curious.

Square de l'Aviation, right in the "Schmatte District" (garment district, literally the "rag trade") of Anderlecht, in the vicinity of the Gare du Midi. David Inowlocki (Daniel Merckx) has his huge showroom nearby. Not too far away from my old address at all, but completely unknown to me up to this moment. Never strayed this way before. A huge Art Deco building, most likely beautiful and striking in its day, now quite passé. The lobby is deserted. The building too, it seems. Not a soul. Eerie feeling. I finally make my way through, all the way to the back. An alley. Disreputable at best. And there is another building there, a rear annex, bigger it seems. Takes some courage to venture ahead. Foul smells of rotting walls, mold, moisture. Not well-lighted. But somehow I get to where I'm going, and I finally meet the slight Mademoiselle Barrette, the archivist with whom I obtained the coveted appointment. And there, lying open just for me on a waiting table, are the four precious relics, the four notebooks the underground devised to record our existence and very being. There had to be a record, it seems. We were real after all, we truly existed. We weren't figments, as the revisionists would have you believe. No one should forget. And the children had to be eventually reunited with their parents. Such foresight. At long last I am staring at my own name "Paul Schwarzbart" with my Anderlecht address, 1 rue des Bassins, and my birth date, 12 IV 33. And also my personal code number "896" -- I was undoubtedly the 896th child registered by this underground cell! And under that number appears my false name "Paul Exsteen". And then my hiding place, "611" to signify the Home Reine Elisabeth, Jamoigne s/Semois, Province du Luxembourg. I cannot help myself: tears are streaming down my cheeks. For myself or for the others? How clever these young résistants were. One needed all four records to make sense of it, and the four were never kept together. Useless to the uninitiated. How clever, how literally foolproof, how ingenious, how incredible! I salute these heroic young men and women who so selflessly gave of themselves to save generations—and so completely succeeded! They who made up the Comité pour la défense des Juifs spirited away some 3000 children from my area, literally all of whom escaped extermination and survived the war. Unfortunately, the same cannot be said for their wretched parents; many of these children were orphaned and never saw their families again. Andrée herself was almost caught; a premonition keeping her from going home one night: the Gestapo were waiting for her in her rooms. One of the notebooks was hidden under a floor board... I shall forever wonder who the young man was, who came to save me. Who he was and what became of him. He must have succumbed, another nameless sacrifice, or he would have attended the reunion we all agree; may he sleep in peace! And be forever thanked.

And suddenly, out of the blue, as I ponder what I am seeing, Mlle Barrette asks me whether I'd be interested in studying my father's file! I almost drop off the chair, she takes me so absolutely by surprise. I could not expect this, for I did not even imagine Papa's file existed, and certainly not right here, in this place. But I am wrong: the files of all the men deported from Brussels are indeed archived here since the Nüremberg trials. Is anyone else aware of this? I've told whoever would listen. There are rows upon rows of files, as far and as high as the eye can see. I am so overcome with emotion that I can hardly breathe. I cannot see too well, either: everything is blurred. And Mlle Barrette does bring me Papa's file, open. And there, on the inside cover, is his passport photograph,

which she detaches and kindly and very simply hands over to me. Bits of paper, neatly hand-or-typewritten, in German, always with all of his particulars... I look at Ken Swartz. Tears are rolling down his cheeks too. I ask him why, since he has already seen so much in his role as film maker, including more recently the killing fields in Asia. "It's this bureaucracy of death! I've never witnessed the bureaucracy of death!" he murmurs, still filming. Indeed! And so I learn what has happened to Papa, after the French deported him East, through Lyon. Auschwitz, and his tattoo, Jude Nr.124951, courtesy of IBM! Years of agony. Then the horrors of Gross-Rosen. Followed by the death march to Weimar Buchenwald, the infamous camp ironically named "Beechwoods" (only the Germans!).

So very few survive the incredible ordeal, but he does, somehow, though his feet are horribly frostbitten. What unbelievable courage, what matchless determination. And finally his demise, probably from the gangrenous wounds on his limbs (the German records state simply "Sepsis" as the cause of death), only about ten days later on 18 February 1945, at 05:30 on a Sunday morning. He is just forty-two years old. He "almost" lives through five years of hell! Incredibly pitiless and heart-wrenching ironies! Barely two months later, on 11 April 1945, the Allies liberate the camp. And the Russians had freed Gross-Rosen on 14 February 1945, only days after the inmates were herded out to their death. No other experience, the reading of that file, holding the life-span of my father in my hands, has so affected and depressed me. I can only hope that no other will, ever...

Walking among rows upon interminable rows of files, breathing in the pungent smells of old paper and the profound sadness of the place, I feel totally shattered. And then we come upon the huge cabinet of Gestapo files, and Mlle Barrette proceeds to show me my family's records, small 4x6 cards, one for each of us, covered with hand-or typewritten information. Almost each one represents a death sentence. I feel like clawing at my hair. Everything so neatly up-to-date, except mine, of course: they still have me living in Anderlecht with my mother; they know nothing about my two-year absence, thank God. That could easily have cost Mutti her life, or much worse. As I always suspected, they could have "plucked" her at any time. But they didn't. So chilling, so horrifying, so mind-boggling. Ken Swartz did indeed give it its rightful name: the bureaucracy of death. I make some off-handed comment, thanking God the Nazis didn't have computers, or none of us would be left standing there. Little do I know as I utter the thought, logical at the time, that IBM was supplying Hitler with all his computer needs throughout the war years via New York and Geneva. No longer just two-faced and fork-tongued France, Switzerland, Sweden... but even America! And today IBM thrives while blatantly disclaiming all responsibility for its treacherous war activities, aiding and abetting the enemy. Traitors to their own country and to humankind, one and all. Where is our government's reaction? Don't they traditionally execute, or at the very least imprison, perpetrators guilty of fighting against their own in time of war? Since they are quite obviously morally bankrupt already, how about a tangible bankruptcy... Where are the lightning bolts of divine justice and retribution? Where is the screaming American eagle? Where is the public outcry of shame and disgust? Where indeed... I totally fail to comprehend! And IBM stock is sought after and still highly regarded.

During one of my subsequent daily phone calls to Gail and the boys, I relate the newly-discovered code numbers to her, mine 896, Jamoigne 611. There is a long silence, then I perceive an almost inaudible whisper: "Honey, please go look at your room door." Well, my door plaque reads 611! I had somehow forgotten. I return to the phone again, and both she and I are choked up for a moment. Though neither one of us really puts much stock in that sort of happening, we are nonetheless shaken by the extraordinary coincidence. And both indeed surprised at being surprised...

Upon my return home to San Rafael, the stressful experience recompenses me with an extremely virulent case of facial shingles. One eye is swollen almost shut. The pain is excruciating. Yet my anguish causes me even deeper suffering. I am now constantly reliving the years past, much more vividly than ever, ever before. I attempt to share, to explain to my dearest wife and sons. The man who just returned is not quite the same man who left, only days before. So much, so much has happened in the short interval. My colleagues and my students must sense the changes too. Our friends the Newmans, Dick and Mary Ann (Dick was best man at our wedding,) invite us to their Sonoma home for a Sunday luncheon. Given the mildness of the day and the early hour when we arrive, they suggest we go for a nice stroll in town before lunch, which we proceed to do. We talk and enjoy one another's company. I'm somewhat uncomfortable, but the drugs are helping to minimize the pain. By and by, we return to their house. Surprise! Half the Tam faculty have assembled there during our absence. It's a big potluck to welcome me home -- and to hear me describe the journey and my experiences, my life's journey. Lots of tears, hugs, camaraderie and affectionate exchanges. Gail sobs uncontrollably. She had never heard some of these details before, for I had not uttered them before. I am essentially giving my first public address on the subject, the first of well over two hundred to-date. Little did I know then. I do feel profoundly compelled to bear witness. Why else did I survive?

The thirty-odd hours of film have to be painstakingly edited and made into a cohesive one-hour-long documentary for television. Ken writes a script and assembles the film, from May to November. I cannot offer my help, since I am the subject, I'm not even allowed to translate. Hence, some glaring errors do creep in. When I visit the broadcasting station on Van Ness Avenue, everyone knows me and calls me by name. The film's release is to coincide with the Kristallnacht anniversary and is aptly titled <u>Shattered Dreams, A Child of the Holocaust</u>. No commercials, just a few public service announcements: the station's VP tells me they consider the film too important to sell. Amazing! On a Friday evening we go on the air, preempting Don Johnson's <u>Miami Vice</u>! And because it is the Sabbath, KRON runs it again the following evening for the Jewish audience that may have missed the initial showing. That does indeed show profound sensitivity on their part! So much for their supposed crass commercialism... Chapeau, KRON!

Gail and I watch the film together and weep in each other's arms. It is incredibly emotional. Marc and David view it downstairs, in their own room. They want to respect our privacy. David says afterwards that even though he gleaned most of the facts over the years, he can now understand and appreciate the actual chronology. He's thirteen years old, and so wise!

The public's response is gratifying and overwhelming Requests for copies arrive in force. Ken responds most generously, making untold copies and sending them out as requested. I'll be forever grateful to him and to his dear wife, Anne. And to KRON TV of course.

The film is widely recognized and rewarded, earning some four Emmys for its makers. And it also receives the Golden Gate Award as "Best Television Historical Documentary" by the International San Francisco Film Festival. At the ceremony, to which Gail and I are kindly invited, I am dragged on stage where, to my absolute surprise and delight, Ken and his colleagues present the award to me. And so I now very proudly and humbly display the symbol of their collective achievement and of their friendship in our home; it's a beautiful memento of our work together. Bob Jimenez, the narrator of the film and KRON News anchor man, subsequently invites us to his home for dinner. First he opens a display case and shows us "Paul's" Emmy, as he calls it. We spend an absolutely lovely evening together, during which he and his beautiful wife could not be more gracious. The tables are turned. Imagine that, he is grateful to me! Complete strangers on the street recognize me, most kindly, though occasionally some do address me excitedly as Mr. Schwarzkopf. I tell them simply that I do not sing! Not always understood: in 1988 the only world-famous Schwarzkopf was the marvelous soprano, Elizabeth. These incidents certainly bring home the awesome power of television. Such memories... and notoriety!

Thereafter, I am in great demand as guest speaker. To-date, schools, colleges, interested organizations, businesses and synagogues invite me, though not a single Catholic church or organization... Staggering: over two hundred venues. Students and their teachers welcome me and write me marvelous letters, some quite inspiring, others wonderfully naive. I travel far and wide; it is clear to me, and to others, that one can and does indeed make a difference... But who will carry on when our voices fall silent? Perhaps someone who heeded our words, be they written or spoken. The now broken silence, however, must never, never prevail again...

XV.

Epilogue

"We, the hidden children of yesterday, are the last generation who witnessed the Holocaust. There were thousands of us in hiding during WWII. Often separated from our parents and siblings, many of us spent years in basements, sewers or concentration camp shadows. In convents or Christian families, we changed our religion and our names in order to survive. While the loss of childhood has cast a long shadow, each of us carries unique memories of this dark period in history. Our stories are too valuable to be forgotten. But until now, our voices have not been heard." (Quoted from the official convention stationery.)

May 26 and 27, 1991. The first, ever, world-wide Hidden Children's Conference: "THE HIDDEN CHILD", the New York City international convention of WWII Jewish children in hiding, sponsored jointly by the ADL and the Child Development Research Center. Of course, that unique experience marks me. These were and continue to be milestone events. Unique. Shattering. Unmistakable.

The Convention underscored and reaffirmed so many thoughts and so many relationships. Some 2000 formerly "hidden" children came to New York from all corners of the world (even

Australia and Korea, the latter a shock to me!) to discuss our past, our present and our future. For many it was their very first opportunity to affirm their true identity and their history. For the 22 from Poland, it was perhaps their first taste of real freedom! I found another "Jamoignard", totally out of contact (as I had been until 1988) with any of us since the Liberation! Then yet another one was recognized... who himself was aware of two more! And so, of the original 83 Jamoigne children, we now know the whereabouts of 61!

Many of the righteous gentiles were recognized and wildly applauded. At one point, the stage was filled with these wonderful human beings who truly exemplify that we are all children of one God and indeed our brothers' keepers!

The two from Belgium, Yvonne Jospa and Andrée Geulen, addressed the convention in plenary session and later the very large Belgian delegation. Reminding us that the world is in great need of our services today, they said that "seeing all their children together made these proceedings the most beautiful days of their lives!" These two ladies and their underground network were responsible for saving some 3000 young lives -- and their ensuing progeny!

There were unbearably painful moments too.

The bulletin boards were covered with little slips of paper and cards, cries of anguish, people still searching for relatives after these 50 years. Some actually found missing links, friends, family, information. The examples are too numerous to mention here, for my mind is spinning still; I returned exhausted, both emotionally and physically, but extremely grateful to have been an integral part of this profoundly moving historical event.

June 1992: Israel, with our Amicale and other friends.

An extraordinary journey, again. We travel together, friends and families this time, very excited by the visit. We Jews are anticipating the joys of "reunion", while our Christian brethren are looking forward to visiting their own holy shrines. So very moving. And we talk, sing, reminisce once again, share. We are indeed a noisy crew. Others will meet us on site.

Jerusalem of Gold. The eternal city, the source of so much belief and history. Breathtaking, unforgettable. Holy. Luxurious hotel accommodations. In a lobby shop, wide-eyed, I find an absolutely gorgeous silk tallit I immediately covet and purchase...

At the Yad Vashem, again, we collect our thoughts and pray together in the crypt housing the names of the death camps. Buchenwald! My Belgian «underground group» and I dedicate trees in the Avenue of the Righteous to honor our extraordinary Christian saviors who were previously presented with the medal of «Righteous Among the Nations» by the Israeli Ambassador to Belgium, the Honorable Avi Primor. We are also here to unveil their personal plaques, and the great honor of dedicating Pol Georis' memorial falls to his godson, me. Later, emerging from the darkness of the children's memorial into stark daylight and glaring sunshine, we sob quietly. I realize with intensely sharp pain that, had my name been among the 1,500,000 continuously read aloud inside, neither Marc nor David would grace this world with their existence!

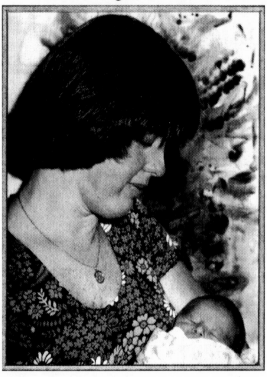

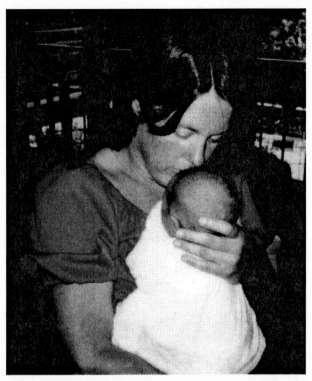

That thought literally tears me up... and I weep bitterly and uncontrollably. Someone I'm embracing very tightly is holding me in his arms too.

In Bethlehem, visiting the Church of the Nativity, we watch in awe as our Christian fellow-travelers weep with excitement and emotion. And we, too, are moved. As we are, anew, watching them at the Jordan, and then once more at the Sea of Galilee. Masada offers them an opportunity to observe our own emotions, again, and again, and again... The Temple Mount, the hills of Jerusalem. So many shrines, so many emotionally-charged moments. The living Bible, the history of our Judeo-Christian civilization, all truly unbelievable, yet so real.

Our last night in Jerusalem, I think, we have a long drawn-out meal at a "Roman" restaurant.

Togas and laurels. Speeches. Michel Goldberg has prepared a long, ponderous one. An historic encounter indeed. I'm anxious, we're all anxious, to get home, but I really don't want to leave here...

New acquaintances, old acquaintances. New memories. I know I shan't ever be able to put Anna Grosfater's melancholy demeanor and far-away, lost look, out of my mind. Her sad face haunts my memory. There are two sets of numbers tattooed on her arm, one above the other; the first is crossed out by a jagged (tattooed) line. I have not seen anything this macabre before or since. When I finally muster enough courage to invade her private space and question her about that extraordinarily painful sight, she willingly relates to me that the Germans at Auschwitz, realizing an "accounting error" had been committed with that particular train of children, ordered the initial markings crossed out and immediately replaced by the "correct" numbers. The oh-so-chilling and ghoulish bureaucracy of death at its very darkest! The Nazis' inhumanity is indeed unfathomable. Every new discovery is worse than what we already knew. There appears to be no end to it... Appalling.

On the occasion of the Third International Gathering of Hidden Children in the spring of 1995, many of us meet again on the expansive campus of the Université Libre de Bruxelles. Another momentous congress, but somehow less "marking" than the first one in New York City. I have often wondered why, and subsequently concluded that perhaps only "firsts" are truly indelible. More reminiscences, new and old acquaintances, new memories. My darling Gail had insisted I come, but she's ill and I'm really more back home with her than here... though I have no inkling as to how ill she really is, nor that she will be gone a year later. Neither does she, I believe. A beloved lady of incredible courage and optimism... ever-present to her family.

Yet another get-together: the 2003 International Conference in the magnificent city of Washington, DC. Well over five hundred "Hidden Children" and spouses convened at the Mayflower Hotel on Connecticut Avenue and spent three charged days together. Not surprisingly, many more girls than boys. A few familiar, though now somehow much older, faces. And a sea of new ones, some affable, some distant or distracted, some indifferent—and a few that clearly wish they were elsewhere. Although Belgium as a country was well represented at this conference, I was indeed the lone boy from Jamoigne: I had to explain, over and over, that I was really Austrian-born and only hidden in Belgium—not truly a Belgian. But what are we, really?

Almost sixty years later, there is still so much agonizing pain. Palpable. Behind the closed doors of the seminars, people open up and break down in sobs. Is there no end to the searching? Just like the initial 1991 meetings: more bulletin boards, more slips of paper (some now computer-generated), more "Have you seen?" "Have you heard from?" And old, old photographs. So infinitely sad, these quiet and yet so piercingly loud screams of utter despair.

But one still senses a remnant, a vestige of hope. And this time again, that surprises me. Shocking.

The group's heart-wrenching pilgrimage to the United States Holocaust Memorial Museum. A brand new exhibit was opened for us, both to honor us and also to celebrate the museum's 10th anniversary: Life in the Shadows. All about hidden children and their rescuers.

My dear Belgian friend Andrée Geulen Herscovici has her photograph and one of her notebooks prominently featured among the rescuers. Deservedly so.

Painstakingly finishing the tour of the permanent exhibits, a rabbi then leads the Kaddish in the starkly beautiful Hall of Remembrance. Memorial candles under the camps' infamous names. Sharry and I light one together, under Buchenwald, the site of Papa's death. Blessed be his memory…

We returned two days later to revisit some of the galleries, such as <u>Life in the Shadows,</u> <u>Daniel's Story,</u> <u>Fighting the Fires of Hate: America and the Nazi Book Burnings,</u> the "<u>Tower of Faces</u>". And finally the Survivors' Registry, where I consulted my mother's, my grandmother's and my own file cards. Remarkable indeed.

Sharry was completely taken with the entire event, her very first of course, and profoundly moved. These are her deeply sensitive reminiscences, beginning with the heart-wrenching "Tower of Faces" of an entire Lithuanian town, the shtetl of Eisiskes (Eishyshok), whose 3,500 Jews were massacred on September 25 and 26, 1941; there were but 29 survivors:

« A whole wall, two whole walls, three stories of photographs, at least twenty feet wide, representing a whole shtetl, a village-worth of beautiful faces, family portraits, all representing people annihilated by the Nazi regime, people who had done nothing to deserve such a fate, people like you and me, as we walk through the museum staring at their innocent faces. "That one looks like my mother, or my sister, or my grandfather, or my aunt or uncle," we hear as we slowly make our way through the faces.

The haranguing voice of Hitler, as we watch video films of swarming crowds marching in a frenzy of approval at his words, his exhortations, his exultation of all things German, "Get rid of the vermin!" And young German faces, open-mouthed and shiny-eyed, looking as avidly ferocious as the snarling, muzzled German shepherd in one poster, held on a leash but eager to do the job he was trained for: terrify and kill. The unimaginable horror of all of this: real because it happened, yet incomprehensible to the heart and soul of anyone with a sense of morality and humanity.

The anger expressed these sixty-some years later by one of the hidden children, a woman whose family was lost, "How could they do this to people who had done no wrong? How COULD they?", echoing in my heart.

Twelve years ago I didn't know much about the children who had been hidden in order to be saved from certain death during the Holocaust, and certainly not that I would now be married to one of those survivors. Hidden children, which meant that their lives somehow were spared, but their childhood, lost. Some were abused, starved, taken in for the money their loved ones or various agencies would pay for their upkeep. Others were in more fortunate circumstances, with some love and attention given to them. All of them experienced the trauma of being ripped in some way from their family at a vulnerable time. One woman spoke of the loss of her family, but also of the loss of her forest: she had been taken in by a forest guardian and spent most of her days from the time she was four until she was six years old alone in the forest, a kind of "wild child". Another told us that her life was a "fairy tale": she was re-united with her family after six years. But by then, she and her brother spoke only French, and her parents German and Polish, and the bond of "family" was no longer there. Each had undergone such different, difficult experiences and now had no common language: the connection was broken. Her brother now lives in a psychiatric care home in Europe, and she goes to visit him once a year. Strangers, who could not live in a circle of love, but merely as co-existing separate beings, their lives broken.

The world-wide meeting of hidden children and spouses in Washington, D.C., August 25-28, 2003. Such a meeting provides a safe haven for people whose experiences have only the thinnest common thread of having been hidden at a vulnerable and formative time in their lives. Vulnerable, and yet most have made a normal or above-average life for themselves. Each had a vastly different set of circumstances, yet the fact of being together makes it possible for them to talk, to tell each other their stories. As a spouse, I was struck by the realization that most of the time, my husband and the others function in a world that knows not of their experiences, and being together in this situation provides the kind of release that brings, if not healing (one man in his seventies is able to cope with other survivors' stories, but kept his own so deeply inside that he cannot speak of it without crying-he was told that tears are good, and he realizes that the only way he will "get past" this event is with his own death), at least the rejuvenation of recognition that one is not totally alone, that grief can be shared.

The deepest feeling I came home with is admiration for the courage of these people, "old" children, one of whom said she is a "channel of life", and that since she was one of only 5,000 Polish Jewish children who survived, she felt she had to make her life meaningful. I have heard my husband speak many times, and one of his lessons is that one person <u>can</u> make a difference. The joy of being alive is what reverberates inside me: how lucky we are to be able to share our lives and continue the struggle to make a difference however we can. »

Prior and subsequent to the meetings, Sharry and I did as many of the "tourist things" we could, in and around Washington, DC. My very first glimpses of our nation's capital. Truly unforgettable: Arlington National Cemetery and the changing of the guard at the Unknown Soldier's tomb, the Capitol, the Lincoln and Jefferson Memorials, Mount Vernon... Such absolutely magnificent national treasures. So proud of being an American!...

Indeed so profoundly grateful and ecstatic to be alive!

A humble witness, bearer of testimony.

"We must never forget that each one of us can and should make a difference. Most Holocaust 'rescuers' made that decision and acted upon it. To stand by is to acquiesce." Paul A. Schwarzbart, 1995

About The Author

Paul Schwarzbart, husband, father, respected teacher, survivor of the Holocaust, was born in Vienna. He fled with his parents when Austria was annexed. He and his mother eventually came to the United States, where he received his undergraduate and graduate degrees at UC Berkeley. His teaching career spanned 45 years. He has spoken over 200 times in various venues recounting his life experiences as a hidden child. In 1988 Schwarzbart's life became the central theme of an award-winning Ken Swartz documentary, *SHATTERED DREAMS, A Child of the Holocaust.*

Printed in the United States
24673LVS00004B/478-528